ONE HUNDRED
KILIMS

ONE HUNDRED
KILIMS
MASTERPIECES
FROM ANATOLIA

Yanni Petsopoulos
Commentary to the illustrations by
Belkis Balpınar

ALEXANDRIA PRESS LTD
in association with
LAURENCE KING

FIRST PUBLISHED IN THE UK
IN 1991 BY

ALEXANDRIA PRESS LTD

IN ASSOCIATION WITH

LAURENCE KING

© 1991
ALEXANDRIA PRESS
121 LEDBURY ROAD
LONDON W11 2AQ
TEL: 071 727 9724
FAX: 071 229 1272

DESIGN: RICHARD FOENANDER

TYPESET IN CENTURY ITC LIGHT
BY BOOKWORM TYPESETTING
IN MANCHESTER, UK

PRINTED AND BOUND BY
AMILCARE PIZZI S.P.A.
IN MILAN, ITALY

BRITISH LIBRARY
CATALOGUING IN PUBLICATION DATA

PETSOPOULOS, YANNI
100 KILIMS: MASTERPIECES FROM ANATOLIA
I. TITLE   II. BALPINAR, BELKIS
746.72

ISBN 1 85669 011 3

Contents

Foreword

This book is dedicated to one hundred admirable kilims, all of them made before living memory, many generations ago. The younger of the kilims illustrated in these pages are fast approaching their 200th anniversary. Yet, at the time these were woven, the older kilims were already of venerable age. This book is equally a tribute to the small group of committed individuals, Herwig Bartels, Johannes Wolff, William S. Taubman and Georgie Wolton, who over many years have assembled magnificent collections, only some of which can be included here. Each followed his or her own vision, but they shared a passion for kilims and spared no effort in their determination to acquire the best examples available. They can all be described as 'first generation' collectors, active long before kilims reached their present level of popularity; indeed Georgie Wolton can probably claim to be the first person ever to collect kilims systematically. To place the vision and achievement of these collectors in context, we need to look back over the last hundred years.

At the turn of the century, the director of the Berlin Museums, Wilhelm von Bode, who can rightly claim to be the father of serious carpet studies, praised the historical and artistic merits of carpets in his opening remarks to the catalogue of the great exhibition of Islamic Art in Munich. As an afterthought he mentioned some distant cousins of these carpets, executed in tapestry weave, but dismissed them as coarse and lacking in artistry. When, three quarters of a century later, in 1979, the first book dedicated entirely to kilims was published, its rapid commercial success demonstrated beyond doubt that attitudes towards kilims had changed dramatically. This change began in earnest in the mid-sixties and can be attributed to a variety of factors, not least the 'hippie' phenomenon.

The 'hippie' generation sought emancipation from post-war conformity; it was a generation of protest. Social 'taboos' were challenged; new lifestyles were established; through music, art, and culture in general, they explored new realms. Far-off cultures, evocative of more ancient, more romantic and more innocent times, caught the popular imagination. All things 'ethnic' became fashionable, kilims included. Colourful, bold and dramatic, they fitted the times. The popularity of this 'ethnic', tribal aesthetic affected knotted carpets as well. During this period there was a shift in taste from the formal, and primarily floral, small-patterned Persian and Turkish carpet, which had dominated Western interior decoration in the first half of this century, to the bold Caucasian, Afghan and Turcoman tribal and village rugs.

Over the next twenty-five years, interest in kilims continued, but, as with all new artistic discoveries, aesthetic appreciation went through certain phases. The first spans the period between 1965 and 1980, when, characteristically, highly decorative Caucasian, Persian, and Afghan kilims with bright colours and bold designs had their heyday. On the Anatolian side, prayer kilims were highly sought after, particularly those related to well known carpet types. In general, the emphasis was on finely woven and intricately patterned kilims with regular designs of the type made in eastern and south-eastern Anatolia (such as those from the regions of Aleppo, Kayseri, Malatya and Erzerum). The only snobbery of this first wave of kilim

aficionados concerned synthetic dyes. If a kilim had natural, primarily vegetal dyes it entered the circle of respectability, and, indeed, during this period there were no significant differences in price or popularity between Thracian, Caucasian, Persian, Afghan, and Anatolian kilims. If anything the latter lagged behind the others.

The second phase, spanning the 1980s, was without doubt the Anatolian decade. Moreover, it was the decade of the dedicated and discriminating collectors of the 'early' kilim. These people started to seek out ever older, rarer and more unusual pieces. Fineness of weave and good condition were no longer important criteria. The closer a particular piece seemed to be to an 'archetype', the more desirable it became. By the end of the decade, so many 'new' types of really old kilims had emerged, that our knowledge of the subject had changed dramatically. What we now call 'collector's kilims' were no longer acquired as floor coverings. Instead, they became – in Bertram Frauenknecht's words – 'Early Turkish Tapestries', with all the positive associations of artistic status the word 'tapestry' implies. Their strong colours and powerful, often irregular designs, redolent of symbolism and abstraction, combined to create a new mystique around them. Thus Anatolian kilims overtook all other categories in popularity among the kilim *cognoscenti.*

Much of the credit for this change in taste belongs to a small group of specialist dealers. Indeed, given the rapid growth in the body of available material during this period, it is not surprising that formal scholarship could not keep pace with the subject. In its absence, connoisseurship took over. Some of these dealer-connoisseurs worked quietly and very privately in influencing the taste of their clients, while others kept a higher profile by organizing many important exhibitions which were usually accompanied by lavish and fully illustrated catalogues.

All these activities enhanced the status of kilims in the carpet community, as became evident at international conferences on oriental carpets, especially during those in London, Vienna and San Francisco, where flatweaves in general, and Anatolian kilims in particular, held an almost predominant position. Indeed, such was the increase in their standing that in January 1990, a three-day symposium dedicated exclusively to kilims was held in Basel. At the same time, kilims started appearing regularly, as a matter of course, in almost every new general book dealing with the subject of oriental carpets. This was a radical departure from the carpet literature available up until the late 1970s. Moreover, the 1980s saw a spate of publications dedicated entirely to flatweaves.

This situation was not without its ironies: when a group of sixteenth-seventeenth century kilims was first discovered in the Ulu Cami, the Great Mosque, in Divriği in the 1970s, they were generally thought of as having classical Ottoman carpet and textile designs. Attitudes towards the status of kilims have since changed so much, however, that in 1988, the noted carpet scholar Charles Grant Ellis published a magnificent Ottoman village pile-rug in the collection of the Philadelphia Museum as a 'kilim-style rug'.

The beginning of this second phase coincides chronologically with the opening of the new Vakıflar kilim museum in Istanbul, located in the outbuildings of the Blue Mosque, the first proper home in Turkey for kilims. Until then, a few, mostly nondescript kilims could be seen at the Ethnographical Museum in Ankara and a few more, similarly unexceptional, at the Turkish and Islamic Art Museum in Istanbul. Nowhere in Turkey was there a systematic and reasonably comprehensive collection open to the public. The new museum was the brainchild of Belkis Acar-Balpınar who, soon after, in 1982, brought out the fully illustrated catalogue of its collection in collaboration with Udo Hirsch.

Just over ten years after the opening of the Vakıflar, at the beginning of the 1990s, another significant breakthrough was made. For the first time, kilims entered the hallowed portals of one of the big art museums in the West, when a major collection of early Anatolian kilims, now known as the Caroline & H. McCoy Jones collection, was acquired by the Fine Arts Museums of San Francisco. The opening exhibition and the publication of a catalogue by its energetic curator Catherine M. Cootner were significant landmarks in the kilim world. Thus for the once-neglected kilim, the decade closed as gloriously as it opened: first with a museum in the East and now with another in the far West.

The popularity of kilims has gone from strength to strength during this period, and this had a direct effect on their commercial value, especially for the handful of pieces considered to be the best and the oldest by a small international coterie of specialized dealers and committed collectors, who vied with each other for every single piece. Whereas, at the beginning of the 1980s, a kilim worth 10,000 dollars made headlines, prices in the range of 30,000 to 50,000 dollars cause no surprises today, and recently, a Turkish dealer asked the 'friendly' price of 200,000 dollars. Such, in fact, is the mystique of these early pieces that an entirely new market has grown up to deal in fragments of kilims mounted on frames and presented as archaeological textiles.

It would now, therefore, be true to say that old kilims are entering a third phase. As is the fate of all recently discovered forms of art, the time comes when the body of previously unknown pieces dwindles, and 'discoveries' such as those made by the first wave of collectors get fewer and farther between. As the San Francisco Museums' acquisition has shown, they will be followed by 'second generation' collections consisting of already known pieces, reflecting the aesthetic choice or the typological focus of their creators, be they individuals or institutions. The age of the 'hunter-collector' is coming to an end; that of the scholar is only just beginning. The 'Undiscovered Kilim' of 1977 has now been discovered.

Kilims:
Terminology and Technique

Today, in popular western usage, 'kilim' is a term applied loosely and indiscriminately to describe all woven floor covers other than knotted pile rugs and carpets. It has become a generic name for fabrics which are executed in a wide variety of techniques such as tapestry weave of all types, weft-float brocading, *soumak* or weft wrapping, warp-faced fabrics, many types of complementary weft-pattern or warp-pattern weaves, and various combinations of all these.

There are, of course, more specific names for many of these fabrics. Here, however, we are faced with a serious problem of interpretation – one which bedevils the entire field of study: does a given term refer to a technique, a design, or indeed to an ethnic, tribal or geographic origin? The answer, except in a few instances, is that we cannot be certain.

For instance, a specific type of weave could have been labelled initially by the name of the place where it had originated. Thereafter, the popularity of that product in the market place would cause the erstwhile toponymic to become a generic label to describe the technique in which it was woven. The term *soumak* is a case in point. It is said to be a corruption of Shemakha, a town in the Caucasus; in some cases it is used to mean Caucasian pieces woven in the area by means of weft wrapping and, more commonly, to describe the technique of weft wrapping in general.

Jijim, or *jajim* is sometimes used to denote weft-float brocaded weavings and, at other times, to denote pieces woven in narrow strips joined together with either brocaded decoration or compound warp-pattern weave. *Zili, zilu,* and *verneh* are other examples where one does not know whether the term is used in conjunction with technique or origin. As for *sileh* it is commonly used to describe a design of angular dragons executed in *soumak*. It is clear, therefore, that no rigorous terminology was ever applied to hand-woven fabrics in the east, and that we cannot rely on any of these terms as anything other than labels.

What then is the proper use of the word *kilim*? Technically, we use it to describe decorated fabrics, mostly made of wool, and woven in weft-faced slit tapestry, which are variously used as coverings and hangings in roles both decorative and functional. However, minor variations aside, the same basic technique characterizes Aubusson and Scandinavian rugs, Gobelin and other European tapestries, South American Precolumbian textiles, North American Navajo Indian blankets, Pharaonic, Coptic or Islamic fabrics from Egypt, Central, South-east Asian and Indonesian weavings and even Chinese K'o-ssu. In some instances the similarity between kilims and these textiles is only structural; in others, however, it extends to designs and, occasionally, to entire compositions. A case in point is the striking resemblance between the Navajo Indian blankets from North America and the 'eye-dazzler' or *baklava*-patterned kilims of the Balkans, Anatolia and Iran. Because of such similarities it would be misleading to define kilims strictly in terms of structure or design. In common usage the term has a definite geographic overtone, being reserved for tapestry-woven rugs, made mainly in south-eastern Europe, the Near and the Middle East. The very same fabrics are sometimes also known by other names such as *gilim* or *gelim* in Persia, and *pala* or *palas* in parts of Anatolia and the Caucasus. In Syria and Lebanon they use the term *busut*, or *b'sath*.

The Structure of Kilims

Tapestry – the technique of weaving used in kilims – is, in its most basic and elementary form, one of the simplest weaving methods, traceable to antiquity and probably to prehistoric times. It could be argued that its beginnings are not very distant from the invention of the loom. To create a tapestry-woven fabric, two types of yarn or thread are required: the warps and the wefts.

Warps

Warps are vertical threads, lying parallel to each other, running the entire length of the kilim. By deciding how many warps are placed on the loom and the spacing between them, the weaver predetermines the width of the kilim. This dimension will remain virtually constant, any possible variation resulting only from unskilled or uneven weaving. The maximum length of the kilim is also fixed by the length of the warp threads, but there is no technical reason why the kilim could not be made shorter if the weaver so decides, either because of a change of mind or a miscalcultation of the length of the desired composition.

Wefts

Wefts are horizontal threads which pass over and under adjacent warps, a sequence which alternates between successive wefts. Practically all kilims are weft-faced fabrics. This term means that the horizontal wefts are beaten down on to each other tightly enough to hide from view the vertical warps. Thus the appearance of the surface of the fabric is owed solely to the wefts, and any patterns are the result of juxtaposing wefts of different colours. Kilims, therefore, have polychrome wefts, while for the invisible warp threads they mostly employ natural, undyed yarns.

The fineness of a kilim is determined by the thickness of the warps and by how closely they are placed, together with the fineness of the wefts and how tightly they are packed. If a kilim is plain and undecorated, or if the decoration is limited to simple, horizontal bands of different colours, it is sufficient to describe it as a *weft-faced, tapestry-woven fabric*. Most kilims, however, abound in complex motifs, rendered in a multitude of colours: here, the coloured wefts forming the decoration do not cross the entire width of the kilim but are confined to the width of their respective design. Such kilims are said to have *dicontinuous wefts*. Description of weft-faced tapestry weave may be elaborated further according to the technique employed to join designs in the diagonal and vertical direction, that is, according to the means of transition at the place of a lateral colour change.

Slit Tapestry

With this technique, where there is a lateral change in colour due to a change in design, each colour returns around the last warp of its respective colour area.

Accordingly, where there is a vertical join, a slit will occur. To achieve a join at an angle, a series of offset slits is woven, creating a stepped outline. The narrower the angle, the less noticeable this is; while the wider the angle, the more pronounced the join becomes. Slits, however, cannot be too long or the resulting fabric would be very weak and prone to tear. Thus kilims woven in slit tapestry do not feature designs with continuous vertical lines; where the weaver needs a vertical join, such as when a side border meets the field, he uses a continuous crenellated line.

Slit tapestry is by far the most common type of weave used in kilims. The resulting fabric is usually double-sided, with the exception of some types of Anatolian kilims where, after completing the weaving of a particular area of colour, the weaver leaves the weft thread loose at the back in order to pick it up and use it further on when the same colour occurs again.

Diagonal Lines, or 'Lazy Lines'

Normally wefts pass across the entire width of their colour area. However, on some kilims where there are wide and large areas of a single colour, the weaver, for ease of execution, only works in small areas at a time. In doing so she returns wefts inside their own colour area, moving laterally one or two warps at a time with each successive weft, to produce an angular outline. By resuming work on the remainder of the colour area, the first part links up with the rest, the resulting join being a diagonal, or 'lazy line', similar in appearance to the diagonal lines produced between adjacent colour zones in slit tapestry. These lines are also occasionally used as a decorative feature to produce variations within a solid area of colour and to enrich the texture of a plain field.

Corrective Wefts

In simple tapestry weave the wefts are horizontal, parallel to each other and perpendicular to the warps. Sometimes, however, either because of the varying thickness of the wool or uneven and occasionally sloppy weaving, the weft line will slope either up or down. To rectify this defect some extra wefts are inserted in a wedge-like fashion. These inserts are known as corrective wefts and, apart from their remedial function, they are often used for decorative purposes in precisely the same way as 'lazy lines'.

Eccentric, or Curved-weft Tapestry

An extension of the principle of corrective wefts forms the basis of a technique used to create curvilinear designs. Instead of inserting the wefts horizontally, the weaver bends them in the shape of the desired design. Successive wefts follow and build up this curve, the shape of which can be altered depending on how tightly or loosely they are packed. At the colour junctions there is no visible structural separation except where there are vertical joins. These are executed in dovetailing which, in fact, forms part of this technique. Some of the smaller designs appear as wedged inserts on a background surface that curves around them, while others are complex interlocking motifs whose outlines merge into one another. A skilful weaver can use this method to produce any kind of curvilinear shape, including a perfect circle. To avoid bulges and produce a fabric which lies flat despite the resulting variation in tension of the wefts, requires a high degree of craftsmanship.

Curved-weft tapestry has been used extensively in Coptic, Chinese and Precolumbian textiles and is ideally suited to kilims with flowing, naturalistic designs. However, because of the constant use of freely-drawn curves and the uneven tension of the wefts, it does not allow for the precise repetition of geometric designs. It is, therefore, not normally used in kilims with primarily angular, rectilinear patterns that can be more accurately and rapidly executed in slit tapestry.

These are the main types of tapestry weaves which occur in kilims. They can be used singly, as in the majority of Anatolian kilims that are woven predominantly in slit tapestry, or in combination. In addition to these basic means of joining areas of colour there are number of other techniques of supplementary decoration employed in the weaving of weft-faced kilims in order to enrich their texture, or to add a multitude of decorative devices on the undecorated parts of their surface.

Weft-float Brocading

This is a technique of applying decoration on top of a foundation surface. The term 'weft float' signifies that the wefts pass over and under the surface of the kilim, forming the design on the front and floating loosely at the back in the spaces between the outline of the design. Weft-float brocading is the sole means of decorating the entire surface of the fabrics we call *zili* or *jijim*. In the case of kilims, weft-float brocading is used only to add small infill designs and border stripes, mostly 'S' or diamond shaped, on plain parts of the finished weft-faced surface. In many cases where the tapestry weave is totally double-sided, these minor motifs are the only way of distinguishing between the front and the back of the kilim.

Weft Wrapping or *Soumak* Brocading

The technique of weft wrapping is commonly referred to as '*soumak*' after the Caucasian rugs of this name which were executed by this method. Weft wrapping can be used directly on the warps as a method of weaving the entire surface of a rug. In the context of normal kilims in weft-faced tapestry, however, weft wrapping is used only as a supplementary brocading technique. It is chiefly employed to hide the joins and, by using a contrasting colour, highlights the outlines of the tapestry-woven designs.

When used in the diagonal direction, one, and more rarely two, rows of wefts are wrapped around the warp at the design junction; when used in the horizontal, the number of rows can be up to four. This process of outlining is usually described inaccurately as overstitching. Normally, the wefts pass over three warps and back under two, creating a continuous chain wrapped around the warps. This ratio of 3:2, however, is not necessarily constant; depending on the shape of the desired design it can also be 2:1, or 4:3.

The Ancestry Of Kilims

Linguistically, the lineage and meaning of the word *kilim* are rather obscure and confusing. In the form we know it, the word comes from Turkey and is defined in modern Turkish dictionaries simply as a 'flat-woven rug'. However, it is absent from Uigur and other early Turkish dictionaries, making its first appearance in the beginning of the 14th century, and then again as a description of garments. The implication is that either the Turks did not weave kilims before they settled in Anatolia, or that they called them something else.

At any rate, the Iranian form, *gilim*, which can be traced back to the tenth to eleventh centuries, seems to provide the immediate origin. It appears in Ferdowsi's great Persian epic poem of the early eleventh century, the *Shah nameh*, a King's book of Kings, and in an anonymous geographical treatise of the late tenth century, the *Hadud al-Alam*, or Frontiers of the World. The word is used specifically for flat-woven covers, blankets and garments, as distinct from floor coverings.

Beyond that, the origins of the word are less obvious. However, woven textiles with phonetically related names appear in a number of mediterranean and western Asiatic languages including Assyrian (*gulinu*), Aramaic (*gelimi*), Hebrew (*gelom*), and Greek (*chlamys*). Another Greek word with a phonetic relationship to *kilim* is *pilima*, a cloth made of felt. Given that felt is probably the earliest man-made fabric, and the relationship between some felt rug and kilim designs, the possibility of a connection is tantalizing.

As for the technique of tapestry weaving which kilims employ, this in its most basic and elementary form is one of the simplest weaving methods. It could be argued, therefore, that its beginnings cannot be very distant from the invention of the loom.

Exactly how far the kilim we know today goes back, however, is a vexed question that cannot be answered unequivocally on present evidence. There is a general consensus that a good number of the old tribal and village kilims of Anatolia that exist today were woven no less than 250 years ago. Many kilim *connoisseurs*, basing themselves on primarily internal comparisons, believe that some must be much older than that.

The earliest surviving kilims, whose dating can be independently corroborated on secure art historical grounds, date back only to the middle of the 16th century. The sophistication of these pieces, which are decorated in a formal Ottoman style, shows such mastery of the technique that there is every reason to believe that they are the result of a long-established weaving tradition. Recent attempts to date kilims using radio-carbon tests have yielded thirteenth and fourteenth century results. Adding to this the evidence of tapestry-woven fragments with geometric designs of hooked medallions and stars found in the Fostat excavations in old Cairo, and some weavings of the Coptic period, one can confidently state that tapestry weaving with designs related to those we find on kilims was practised extensively in the eastern Mediterranean throughout our era.

In the fifth century BC, while listing the riches of the court of Cyrus, Xenophon

Originality in the Context of Symbolic Art

When we look at the work of great painters, and in particular at 20th century abstract works, our natural reaction is to try to fathom the artist's mind, to get to grips with his personal interpretation of man, nature, objects or ideas. The further removed they are from naturalism, or academic realism, the more we are led to think in terms of an artist's individual creativity and originality.

By education and conditioning, we tend to react along similar lines whenever we are first exposed to a hitherto unfamiliar form of art from a different culture. Early Anatolian kilims are no exception. The strength and contrast of their colours, and their bold, abstract designs elicit a similar response, and we tend to apply the same criteria in trying to understand them. We see in them patterns and designs forming elaborate compositions. In some we find a rich complexity of intricate, interrelating ornaments, while in others designs are used sparingly to produce highly abstract and strikingly simple effects. Our initial attraction is purely visual.

Prolonged acquaintance and a close-focus examination, however, reveal an entirely different picture. Despite the seemingly countless varieties of kilims, certain designs occur again and again. They combine in a formal, structured manner to form sequences or patterns, and almost all belong to a number of distinct compositional types.

Indeed, some early kilims are so similar to one another, down to small details (plates 2 & 4, 57 & 58, 86 & 89), that one might be forgiven for thinking that they are mere copies of each other. Yet, there are always differences between them, be it a subtle change in scale, or in colour balance. Each is the individual expression of a time-honoured archetype, showing its creator's skill while closely adhering to tradition. Originality in this context has the opposite meaning: it implies using one's skill to keep faith with the roots of tradition. Indeed, the closest modern man in the West comes to understanding art in the manner of traditional societies is in his appreciation of a performance of classical music. In other words, traditional art should be seen in the same light as the interpretation of a given piece of music by conductors and soloists, rather than as the individualistic creation of a modern painter.

This strict adherence to originals would be pointless and sterile if the archetypes were no more than meaningless patterns, however beautiful. The opposite is certainly the case. The vocabulary of kilim decoration is rich in symbolism. So much so, that it would not be out of place to speak in terms of an iconography of kilim ornament.

In seeking to understand the symbolic meaning of kilims, it is of paramount importance to understand that the entire composition, and even the structure, is a symbol. The synthesis of patterns and designs which form the composition does not derive from the juxtaposition and combination of heterogeneous and haphazardly chosen elements. In other words, the kilim is not just the sum of its parts. All the elements of decoration are harnessed within the overall composition, whether they are individual designs, or sequences of designs forming patterns, which in turn create compositions. Certainly, each element has its own place and its own role to play. But that role is as part of a totality and should not be seen or judged in isolation. Attempting to understand designs in isolation would be tantamount to removing a key word from a well-constructed sentence and expecting its meaning to remain unchanged.

Modern man has been largely conditioned by his environment and education to examine the world rationally. The process of intellectual analysis is ill-suited, however, to the task of finding the key to the meaning of symbols. Such a process can only lead to a superficial recording of their appearance and to comparisons of their visual development geographically, chronologically and also in terms of the use they were put to and of the medium of their expression. The dangers of over-generalization and over-simplification inherent in this approach are great, and relationships can be assumed which are totally artificial, such as that a cross found on a kilim might be proof of its Christian origin.

Symbols are the means of expressing eternal and universal truths, not personal or subjective opinions and tastes. Whether they are understood intellectually or not is immaterial; they are interpreted intuitively rather than by rational analysis. Their significance is accepted, not judged. 'I am the flute, Lord, Thine is the music', said Rumi, the great thirteenth-century mystic from Konya, thus expressing with poignancy the essence of symbolic, 'mystical' art and the relationship between the craftsman and his work.

What Rumi described so beautifully, is the law of correspondence which holds that what is below is a reflection of what is above. This is the cornerstone of all symbolism, for a symbol is the reflection of a higher reality on a lower plane. The weavers of kilims followed this concept to the letter; their ubiquitous use of designs in mirror image bears ample testimony to this.

While it is in the nature of symbols to have a certain degree of universality, once adopted by a tradition they are assimilated in it and, their origins being forgotten, they become an inalienable part of it. In this process of adoption, symbols which contain multiple layers of meaning may be stripped of some of them and, occasionally, invested with new ones. For instance, the prayer arch or *mihrab* of Islamic architecture is derived from the much more ancient cult motif of the niche, yet when we see it on a kilim or carpet, we automatically associate it with the ritual of Moslem prayer. Sometimes symbols can undergo an important shift of emphasis either downwards or upwards within the same tradition. Take for example the role of icons in the art of eastern Christianity, before, during and after iconoclasm.

In the study of any traditional art form, the symbolic designs used in its decorative repertoire must be examined first and foremost for the meaning they held within that tradition. Only as a secondary consideration is it necessary to extend the search for their meaning further. This second stage only concerns the fuller understanding of the individual symbol rather than the meaning it has within the art form under scrutiny. Where a symbol first appears may well be very interesting. This, however, does no more than satisfy curiosity.

Thus, different uses of the same symbols by different cultures in no way invalidate or contradict one another. The specific meaning of a symbol only reflects the spiritual beliefs of the particular tradition using the symbol, and efforts should be concentrated on understanding symbols in that context. For this kind of understanding, however, participation in the tradition which used these symbols is absolutely essential, and for most of us, this is a goal beyond reach.

In the study of the early Anatolian kilim, however, the problem can be set in a much narrower perspective. The question is not whether kilim ornamentation can be symbolic or not, since there is no doubt that in traditional art symbolism is ever-present in all methods of expression. Rather, it is a matter of finding out which of the kilims are a true expression of traditional art and which are not, and of finding a key to understanding them.

With more recent kilims, those woven a hundred years ago or less, at a time when the the hitherto continuous chain of tradition broke under the strain of external influences incompatible with its own level of reality, the time came when the once-obvious symbols became so stylized that they underwent a gradual loss of meaning, which, in turn, led to a rapid and natural degeneration in form. Unfortunately, this process of degeneration acquires an accelerating momentum, and it takes a surprisingly short time (often as little as a single generation) to reach a situation where weavers no longer comprehend either the significance or the importance of the designs they use. This lack of understanding, deplorable as it may be, would not by itself have been fatal, since symbols, as mentioned earlier, do not have to be understood intellectually in order to be valid. However, by looking upon them merely as decoration, the weavers felt free to alter the size, shape and colour of their designs and to arrange them eclectically in new patterns, creating different compositions, thus disrupting forever the links with the past.

This process of degenerative evolution, which has by now reached all kilim-producing areas, was by no means uniform, nor did it happen simultaneously. Certain areas resisted change longer and more strongly than others. This resistance seems to be directly related to inaccessibility. It follows that urban centres were the first to sever their links with tradition. It may be argued that with pile carpets this process began many centuries ago, in the ateliers of Ottoman Turkey and Safavid Persia, with the adoption of court inspired and imposed styles for the execution of large commercial orders, or royal commissions for palaces or mosques. In the case of kilims, however, as the production remained largely in nomad and village hands, degeneration did not start in earnest until the second half of the last century, and did not become widespread before the First World War.

Technique and
Design Interdependence

From the moment man tried to reproduce nature or communicate ideas by means of visual symbols, we have the beginnings of the formation of art. Leaving aside his sources of inspiration, on the level of execution, an artist has two basic options for decorating a surface. The first, which is by far the simplest, is like putting pen to paper: a design is applied directly to an existing surface, as in wall or pottery painting, and engraving on wood or metal. Such methods of decoration are, therefore, called direct processes. An indirect process, as the word implies, is one where the visual result is arrived at gradually by the simultaneous creation of the structure of which it forms part. Most decorated textiles fall within this category, at the most basic level of which we have patterned felts.

The formation of settled agricultural and pastoral societies brought with it the need to develop skills and techniques to exploit the byproducts of farming and animal husbandry. An early breakthrough in this direction was the invention of the loom. Starting with plain weave, it did not take long for weavers to realize that they could use yarns of different colours to produce a decoration of stripes or bands. As we have already seen, the next step was the use of discontinuous wefts to allow the build-up of patterns within these bands. The result is tapestry – the technique of weaving used to this day in kilims.

When dealing with the material output of a culture and its decorative vocabulary we often find that the same forms or designs are transferred from one medium to another. Such a transference seems to be subject to a hierarchy. For example, when a ceramic and a metal vessel have the same shape, but what is a decorative feature in one is a structural requirement in the other, we naturally conclude that the shape of the former is borrowed from the latter. Conversely, when the same decorative motifs are executed in a direct process like painting and in an indirect process such as embossed or *repoussé* metalwork, we assume that the latter derives its inspiration from the former.

A similar instance of transference which raises the question of hierarchy, is the relationship between certain types of Anatolian kilims and the reed screens used in the *yürts*, the round felt tents of the central Asian Türkmen.

Both Belkis Balpınar and Josephine Powell have pointed out the similar use to which kilims and reed screens are put, their comparable sizes, and the many common decorative elements between the two. The typical screen, as we know it today, is placed along the perimeter wall of a round tent. It is made up of either juxtaposed reed stems, or thin bunches of hay, wrapped in wools of different colours, to produce complex interlocking designs. Where the motifs go in a diagonal direction, they create a pronounced stepped outline, the size of each step being governed by the thickness of the reed. This is a perverse and laborious composite process, which in absolute terms must, therefore, be of later origin than the more basic slit tapestry weave.

Nevertheless, a good case can be made for certain kilim designs deriving from those on reed screens. This is most immediately obvious in a recently discovered group of old kilims woven in southern Anatolia, in the region near Antalya (plates 27–30). The designs of these kilims have a similarly pronounced stepped outline, the steps and slits echoing in scale the thickness of the individual reeds of the screens. Balpınar goes on to propose an ethnic connection between them as well, suggesting a central Asian Kazak, or Kırgız Türkmen origin for the weavers of these kilims.

Interestingly, Arabic may provide an indirect indication of the origin of the connection between these screens and kilims. The term for the tapestry woven kilim in Syria and Lebanon is *busut*, or *b'sath*. The intriguing possibility arises that this derives from the Greek *psatha*, which has a dual meaning: it describes a method of weaving not unlike the tapestry weave of kilims, as well as the finished product, a mat made of reed leaves, grass, or straw.

The Decoration of Kilims: Concepts and Motifs

As we have just seen, the earliest and most elementary method of decorating a tapestry-woven fabric is to divide its surface into plain bands of different colours. Altering the widths of the bands gives rise to an infinite variety of sequences of wide panels alternating with narrow bands, and even narrower stripes. The next step is to introduce decoration into some or all of these bands. This can take the form of a large single motif (plate 3), a series of smaller repeated motifs (plate 25), or continuous patterns (plate 90). Such is the atavistic attachment of Anatolian weavers to the distant past, that thirty-seven out of the hundred kilims illustrated here follow this ancient format of decoration. Freeing the weavers' minds from the discipline of the bands, to enable them to treat the entire surface of the kilim as a single unit or 'canvas', is conceptually a 'later' development.

It should be pointed out here, that the typically long and narrow Anatolian kilim was meant to be viewed with its long side (the direction of the warps) on the horizontal. The decorated bands were, therefore, vertical. It should consequently be apparent that the weaving of Anatolian kilims is a doubly indirect process. Not only are the designs and their background built up simultaneously through the juxtaposition of blocks of contrasting colours, but as the weaver progresses along the direction of the warps, she has to remember that what is being created is at 90 degrees to the direction in which it is meant to be viewed. At least eighty of our hundred kilims conform to this process, and are meant to be viewed perpendicularly to the direction of the weave.

Having taken into account the physical imperatives imposed by the medium we should turn our attention to some of the main principles governing the decoration of kilims.

Symmetry and Reciprocality

Symmetry, or 'symmetricization' as Cathryn Cootner chooses to call it, is a feature prevalent on most kilims. It can be applied to individual motifs, arrangements of motifs or to entire compositions, along one or both of its axes.

Symmetry is perhaps the single most important principle of layout used by the weavers of Anatolian kilims. The term should not be understood in its modern, absolute sense, as many of these kilims at first sight look anything but symmetrical. Rather, it should be thought of as a concept allowing us to understand the way individual motifs as well as entire compositions are built up. It can be applied on either the horizontal axis (plates 2 & 3) or the vertical (plates 22 & 47), but occasionally along both (plate 17).

This abstract concept becomes easier to visualize when we think in terms of an image and its reflection in water. In one form or another, such 'mirror images' appear on the vast majority of the pieces illustrated in these pages (83 out of 100) and testify to their symbolic nature, since as we have already mentioned, symbolism is based on the law of correspondence which holds that what is below is a reflection of what is above, a reflection of a higher reality on a lower plane.

The second most important layout characteristic is reciprocality. Visually, this effect is created in a number of ways. First, when the spaces between motifs have the same value as the motifs themselves. This is a very regular principle governing the relationship between the ground and the borders. Sometimes, at the junction between the central ground and the borders a simple reciprocal outline is created (plates 13, 59 & 73) while in others, the two interlock (plates 54, 67 & 98).

As for reciprocal motifs, they can either be juxtaposed with their mirror image, a typical occurrence when the decoration is arranged in bands (plate 39), or when they interlock, causing the eye to question which is the design and which is the background (plates 55 & 65).

This brings us to the phenomenon we describe as a field-pattern illusion. This is well illustrated by plates 52, 53 and 54. The two rows of white hooked motifs on plate 54 seem to float on a blue background. On plate 53, however, the arrangement of the ground in bands allows us to see either box-like medallions on a white ground or the two rows of white hooked motifs on a banded background. Plate 52 seems to settle the argument by showing them separately as designs in their own right.

Continuous reciprocal pattern at the colour junction between field and border, creating a visual balance between the two.

Motifs and their background with equal value, creating an ambiguity as to which is the pattern and which is the field.

Another version of the field-pattern illusion, where the spaces between the motifs create complementary motifs.

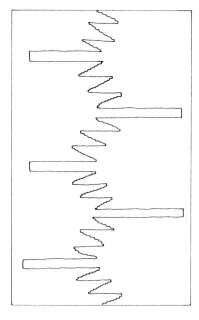
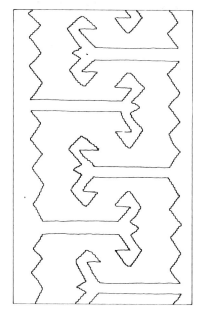
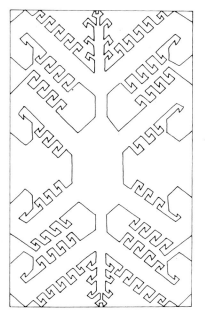

Field-pattern illusions demonstrate a skillful weaver's ability to exploit fully and deliberately the possibilities afforded by the technique of tapestry weave in which designs and background are built up simultaneously. On the level of execution, reciprocal patterns are relatively easy to memorize because of their rhythmic character. On a higher plane, however, they represent all manner of positive-negative and male-female forces in equilibrium.

Anatolian kilims contain countless motifs to which these decorative concepts apply. A cursory examination of a few of the most important allows us a further insight into their weavers' creative process.

The Niche

The motif of the arched niche is a potent symbol which appears in many early cultures. In some cases it denotes a place of honour for a deity or a ruler, while in others it is associated with a window or doorway to paradise.

While in later kilims, those woven over the last 150 years, single-niche examples (prayer kilims) abound, one would be hard pressed to identify more than a handful of pieces which might perhaps predate 1800. Yet in 'early' Anatolian kilims

A. Directional niche (head and shoulders type).

B. Superimposed directional niches.

C. Directional niche.

D. Directional niche.

E. Niche combined with its mirror image.

F. Double-sided niche motif forming an elongated cartouche.

G. Condensed double-sided niche motif in the form of a hexagonal medallion.

H. Double sided niche motif and its mirror

image arranged as a pair of hexagonal medallions.

I. A band flanked by niche-like motifs acting as border devices.

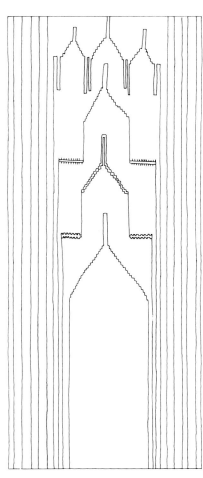
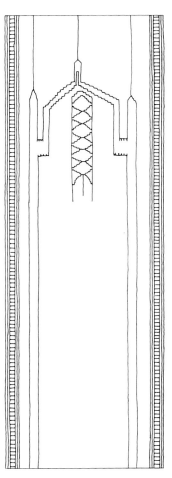

A   B   C

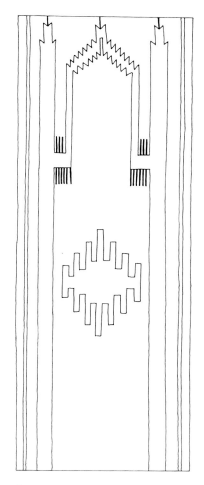

D

E

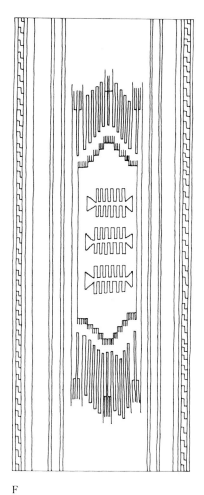

F

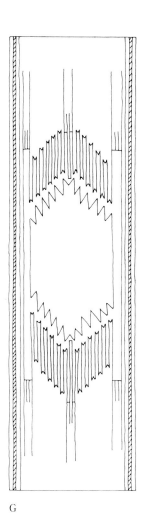

G

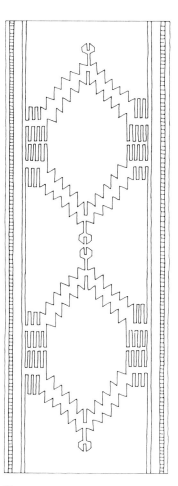

H

I

the niche form used in repetition is among the most popular compositions. They are mostly juxtaposed in a band format (plates 1, 6 & 85), and less frequently they are superimposed (plates 45 & 50).

The interpretation of multiple-niche kilims as *saffs*, rugs with multiple Islamic prayer arches (*mihrabs*), is an overlay to earlier symbolic meanings and demonstrates how a living tradition was able to incorporate new concepts by re-interpreting its own thematic repertoire.

The various stages of transformation the niche form underwent in the hands of weavers offer an insight into the process by which motifs are interpreted. Starting with the directional niche (plates 1 & 6), the motif is combined with its mirror image into a long cartouche (plates 4, 7, 9 & 63). This cartouche is then condensed to look like a hexagonal medallion (plate 3). The principle of the mirror image is now applied to the 'medallion' which thus appears repeated within a band twice (plates 36 & 64), or even three times (plate 61).

The shape of the niches in some kilims closely resembles the head-and-shoulders form of Anatolian tombstones (plate 85). This may be connected with the old funerary custom in parts of Anatolia to use kilims as shrouds for wrapping the bodies of the dead prior to burial.

The Tree of Life

The tree is one of the oldest symbols of life and of the ideal world. It shares with the niche an association with paradise and the after-life. Indeed, many cultures combine the two by placing a tree within a niche. In the context of early kilims, we do not seem

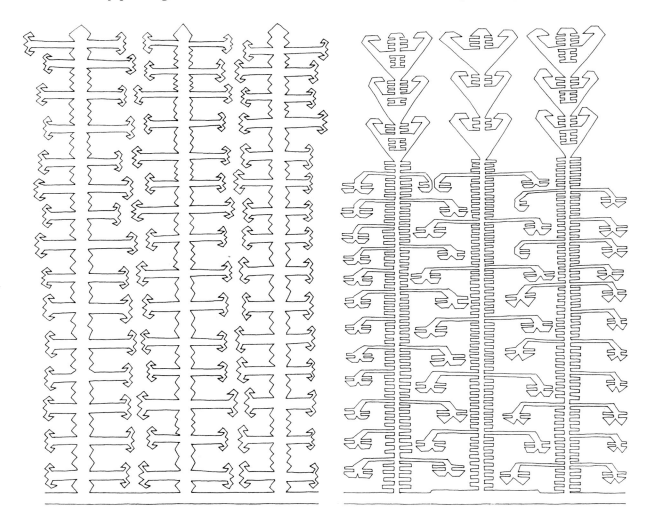

to find trees on the large, long and narrow Anatolian pieces. They appear instead on kilims of a squarer format, and unlike the various niche types, the trees always grow in the direction of the weave along the warps. The use of this motif seems to be concentrated in the southern Balkans, and in north-western Anatolia, in kilims woven by the Yüncü tribes (plates 21 & 22).

Elibelinde

Literally 'hands on hips', the *elibelinde* is a representation of a female figure. In its most basic form the motif consists of a triangular base representing the body, a small diamond at its apex representing the head, and a pair of incurving hooks representing the arms. It is thought of as a symbol of fertility, the origins of which go back to the neolithic cult of the Mother Goddess. Paradoxically, despite the Goddess connection which is deemed to be of Near Eastern origin, the motif is favoured by Türkmen tribal weavers whose ancestors came from much further east.

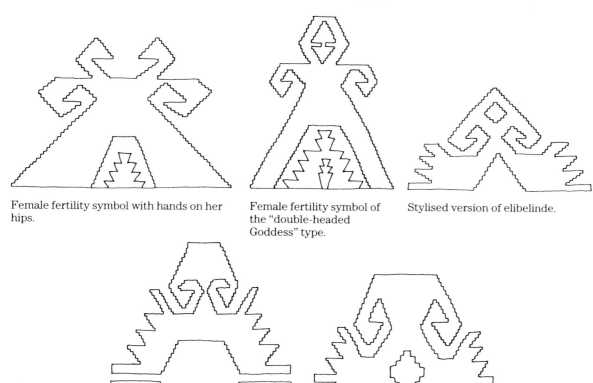

Female fertility symbol with hands on her hips.

Female fertility symbol of the "double-headed Goddess" type.

Stylised version of elibelinde.

The elibelinde and its mirror image combined into a single motif.

The elibelinde motif with its mirror image.

Like the niche, the *elibelinde* is combined in any number of ways. Thus we have directional *elibelinde* with one head (plates 69 & 81) and others with two heads (plates 9 & 39). Then again we find the *elibelinde* motif doubled-up in mirror image along the base. In some instances the two halves are clearly distinct (plates 37 & 68), while in others they are joined up to form a single motif (plates 33 & 34).

Twin Horns

Hooked motifs combined in pairs, and referred to by weavers as ram's or bull's horns, symbolize the male figure. Unlike female representations, these seldom appear on their own as the main field designs. They appear instead in conjunction with the female motifs with which they are often interlocked, in a field pattern illusion, one forming the background to the other (plate 78). This is especially noticeable in kilims whose main motif is the supine, birth-giving Goddess (plates 94, 95 & 99). Horned motifs appear regularly, however, on side borders (plate 54), and on end borders or dividing bands (plates 59 & 61).

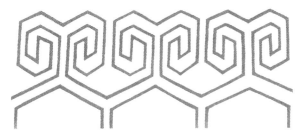

Twin horn motifs as part of the field decoration.

Twin horn motifs as part of a border pattern.

Baklava

The decoration of some kilims consists of small rhomboidal blocks of colour, the juxtaposition of which forms eyedazzling patterns with saw-tooth edged, serrated outlines. In Anatolia this pattern is called *baklava* after the eponymous Turkish pastry which is made in large trays and cut into similar rhomboidal shapes. *Baklava* decoration can be used to create diamond-shaped medallions (plate 41), to decorate bands (plate 92), or to cover the entire surface of a kilim (plate 51).

The baklava motif used as a pattern of overall decoration.

The baklava motif used to form a star-shaped medallion.

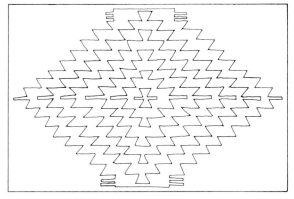

Comb-like and *Parmaklı* Motifs

Literally 'with fingers' or more loosely 'finger-like', the term *parmaklı* is used by weavers to describe a method of decoration in which the outlines of individual designs and border patterns consist of a continuous series of tapering, finger-shaped protrusions.

Parmaklı protrusions appear on a wide variety of western Anatolian kilims where they are used to produce a great number of different visual effects (plates 42-43 & 46-49). Along with *baklava* patterns, some forms of *parmaklı* decoration are the only aspects of the Anatolian decorative vocabulary to be found in Şah Savan kilims from western Iran.

A more geometricized and rectilinear version of the *parmaklı* protrusions produces a comb-like, denticulated outline. This is most often found on small hexagonal or diamond-shaped medallions which are commonly used as infill motifs (plates 5, 13, 83 & 84). Such protrusions, however, are also used effectively in border patterns (plates 44, 87 & 89).

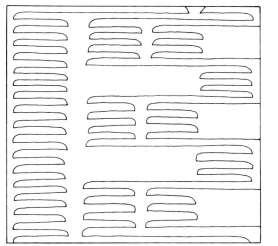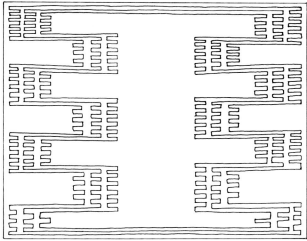

Variations on the use of parmaklı and comb-like motifs

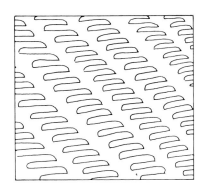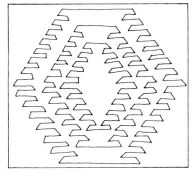

Colour and Pattern

Where a single motif is repeated over the entire surface (other than in bands), depending on how the colours are arranged, different patterns are created, such as chevrons (plates 83 & 84), diagonal bands (plates 32 & 33), lozenges (plates 38, 51, 66 & 68), and more rarely vertical bands (plates 37 & 46).

No mention of the use of colours in Anatolian kilims, however, is adequate if it fails to state emphatically how crucial they are to the finished product. Whatever a weaver's technical skills, the result would have been a pale shadow of itself without the sometimes subtle and sometimes shockingly brutal brilliance of the colours the Anatolian flora provided for them.

The subject of patterns, designs and their colour combinations is inexhaustible. In many instances, however, contemplation is more rewarding than analysis, the Anatolian weavers of old never ceasing to surprise and delight us with their inventiveness in re-interpreting in a myriad of ways the symbolic language of their ancestors and of their land.

Commentary to the Plates

1 Western Anatolia
The Galveston Collection
0.79 × 2.60 m

'*Saff*' kilims with directional, multiple niches are very rare in Western Anatolia. Nevertheless, the texture and the colours of this early piece, as well as the use of white cotton, indicate it might have been woven somewhere in the region between Denizli and Afyon, probably in or around Dazkırı. The weft-twined ornamentation in the narrow stripes between the niches are also a typical feature of this region.

For the iconography of multiple-niche, '*saff*' kilims see: J. Mellaart, U. Hirsch, B. Balpınar, *The Goddess from Anatolia*, Milan 1989, vol. IV, pp. 33–41, figs. 32–37 and B. Balpınar, 'Multiple-niche kilims within their historical context' in Jürg Rageth ed, *Anatolische Kelims, Symposium Basel, Die Vorträge*, Basel 1990, pp. 83–93.

This fragmentary piece has five and a half directional niches. In Islamic tradition, the number of things must be single, because God 'Allah' is single, but this kilim had at least six niches, as does the red and blue '*saff*' in the Fine Arts Museums of San Francisco (C. M. Cootner, *Anatolian Kilims, The Caroline & H. McCoy Jones Collection*, London 1990, p.90, pl. 1).

2 North-western Anatolia
Georgie Wolton
1.77 × 2.64 m

Comparing this kilim to the very similar one on plate 4, two main differences emerge. The four red niches floating against uniformly green bands in plate 4, are placed here alternately on blue and green grounds. Moreover, in plate 4 the series of narrow stripes dividing the main bands are all woven in tapestry, while some of the similar bands here are enriched with a continuous row of 'S' motifs in weft-float brocading.

PUBLISHED:
From the Danube to the Euphrates, Kilims of the 18th and 19th Centuries, Athens 1990, cat. no. 14.

3 North-western Anatolia
Private Collection, New York
1.53 × 2.90 m

This piece shows another local variant of the same double-sided niche composition. The four elongated double-sided red niches of plates 2 & 4 which contain three bird-like motifs, appear here shortened, as plain red hexagonal medallions with a saw-tooth outline. This piece is woven in one of the native or semi-nomadic villages in the mountainous region around Kelez south of Bursa. There is a closely related but larger piece in San Francisco, where the niches float against blueish-green bands, instead of the dark indigo blue used here (see: C.M. Cootner, *Anatolian Kilims, the Caroline & H. McCoy Jones Collection*, London 1990, pl. 14). Another comparable piece is published in H. Ploier, *Gewebte Poesie, Sammlung Konzett*, Graz 1991, pl. 74.

4 North-western Anatolia
The Galveston Collection
1.58 × 2.70 m

This kilim, which compares very closely with the piece on plate 2, is woven in the villages around Kelez, south of Bursa. Its structure, with goat hair warps, its saw-tooth selvedge pattern, and its composition of bands containing multiple medallions in the form of double-sided niches in mirror image, is typical of kilims woven in some of the native and semi-nomadic (*yerli, yörük*) villages in this mountainous region.

Two more similar pieces are published in: B. Frauenknecht *Anatolische Kelims*, Nürnberg 1982, pl. 4, and in J. Eskenazi & D. Valcarenghi eds., *Kilim Anatolici*, Milan 1985, pl. 27.

5 Western Anatolia
The Galveston Collection
1.77 × 3.10 m

To my knowledge, the composition of this highly unusual kilim is unique. It may have been woven somewhere around Çal, north of Denizli in western Anatolia. The uncommonly wide end borders, consisting of plain red and brown stripes, emphasize the ornamented centre, in which a large eight-pointed star is superimposed in the middle of a staggered pattern of comb-like, denticulated diamond medallions.

The utilization of a single central medallion is very rare in Anatolian kilims. Its form, too, is unknown elsewhere in tapestry-woven kilims. However, the weaver of this kilim might have been influenced by a group weft-float brocaded rugs, *zili*, woven south of Denizli, where much smaller stars, with a similar eight-pointed outline and a quartered square in the centre, are used as an overall pattern of decoration.

To resolve the problem of long slits on the vertical straight lines of the large star, inherent in weft-faced, tapestry weave, the weaver has resorted to the use of warp sharing, a technique known as 'dove-tailing'. While common in Ottoman and Persian 'Court' kilims, as well as on some west Persian village and nomadic pieces, this feature is very rare in traditional kilims from Anatolia. As far as I know, it is only found in a unique red-ground kilim in the Vakıflar Kilim Museum, in Istanbul. (See J. Mellaart, U. Hirsch, B. Balpınar, *The Goddess from Anatolia*, Milan 1989, vol. I, p. 19, fig. 10.)

6 Central Anatolia, Cappadocia
Private Collection, Cologne
1.27 × 2.11 m

Though similar in composition to plate 1, and sharing with it the use of supplementary weft-float brocading in the narrow bands, this kilim could not be more different in terms of colour and texture. Here the weave is extremely fine and the colours bright and saturated. The difference extends to the design; the proportions of the top of the niches here are much smaller than those on the '*saff*' on plate 1.

As this magnificent kilim has lost both its ends, there is no way of telling how many niches it had originally. There is, however, a related but probably later piece with darker colours in Georgie Wolton's collection in London which is complete, and has ten niches. The sombre colour scheme of this last piece compares closely with a worn one-niche fragment in San Francisco (C.M. Cootner, *Anatolian Kilims, the Caroline & H. McCoy Jones Collection*, London 1990, pl. 10).

Therefore, while superficially similar, the variation in colours and weave among the few surviving examples suggests that the use of this particular variant of the '*saff*' design was not confined to any one area of Anatolia. As for this particular kilim, it must have been woven in Cappadocia in the region between Niğde and Bor. With its very fine structure and colours, it is also related to silk garments and furnishings woven in slit-tapestry kilim technique in the

Aleppo region in Syria. Indeed, this type of '*saff*' kilim may have been woven by weavers who were once in Aleppo, and then re-settled in different parts of Anatolia by the Ottoman government.

7 Central Anatolia, Cappadocia
Georgie Wolton
1.46 × 3.26 m

This kilim must have been woven in the valley between Urgüp and Niğde in Cappadocia. While sharing with the previous pieces from north-western Anatolia the concept of double-sided niches, the interpretation and execution of the design in these Cappadocian pieces is very different, as are the colours. The ground colour is usually white, and the niches contain a pair of denticulated diamond medallions. A distinctive peculiarity of these kilims is the comb-like termination of the intermediary striped bands. An example with the same feature, and a similar treatment of the pointed arches, is published in J. Mellaart, U. Hirsch, B. Balpınar, *The Goddess from Anatolia*, Milan 1989, vol. I, p. 89, fig. 10. This, however, has six against the seven niches here, and they are flanked by a series of three narrow end borders with different repeat designs. Yet another appears in C. Cootner, *Anatolian Kilims, the Caroline & H. McCoy Jones Collection*, London 1990, pl. 9 but, unlike this piece, is woven in two halves.
ILLUSTRATED:
D. Waterhouse, 'Orphans of the art world', *HALI*, vol.7, no. 2, 1985, p.23.

8 Central Anatolia
Georgie Wolton
1.68 × 3.15 m

This strong and austere kilim must have been woven in the Karaman region, southeast of Konya. A similar composition, richer in colour and with the tops of the niches squared off in mirror image, can be seen in Cootner, 1990, pl. 3. In contrast, this one has angular, pointed niches. The colourful, narrow bands with a reciprocal pattern dividing the former are replaced here with bands of diamonds.
ILLUSTRATED:
D. Waterhouse, 'Orphans of the art world', *HALI*, vol.7, no. 2, 1985, p. 23

9 Western Anatolia
The Galveston Collection
1.36 × 3.25 m

The individual design elements, the colours and the structure of this kilim suggest it must have been woven by Saçıkara *yörüks* in the region around İsparta, Denizli or Burdur.

As on plates 2, 3, 4, 7 & 8, the main element of the composition is the double-sided niche in mirror image. Here, however, the niches have a distinctly different character. They take the form of elongated cartouches terminating in pairs of hooked ornaments which are separated from each other by narrow patterned bands. This interpretation of the double-sided niche appears more often in kilims woven much further east (plate 63).

A kilim of very similar origin is published in H. Ploier, *Gewebte Poesie, Sammlung Konzett,* Graz 1991, pl. 68. There, however, the double-sided niches are confined to the centre and are flanked by two wide skirts of a pattern related to plate 11.

The reciprocal motif in the large end borders consists of a skirt-like triangle topped with a pair of incurving arms and two 'hook' heads. This design is known as *elibelinde,* hands-on-hips, a symbol whose origins may be found in the goddess figures of ancient Anatolia (For a discussion of the *elibelinde* symbol, see: J. Mellaart, U. Hirsch, B. Balpınar, *The Goddess from Anatolia,* Milan 1989, vol. IV, pp. 43-48, figs. 58–79).

10
Western Anatolia
Private Collection, Cologne
1.65 × 3.04 m

Like plate 9, this kilim was probably woven by Saçıkara *yörüks* between İsparta and Konya, near Lake Eğridir, perhaps in Gelendost.

Though similar in composition to plate 9, the niches in this kilim are filled with pairs of hooked ornaments, and are separated by brown bands containing rows of colourful four-hook motifs of a type found throughout Anatolia (plates 87, 88, 91, 92 & 93).

11
Western Anatolia
The Galveston Collection
1.66 × 3.03 m

The profusion of scattered small motifs and the rows of stars within hexagons in the dividing bands are typical of the kilims woven in or around Çine in the province of Aydın in western Anatolia. This piece must have been woven there by Saçıkara people. This explains the dense use of small patterns so characteristic of the kilims from Maraş in south-eastern Anatolia, as that region is also peopled by the Saçıkara. When looking at the long side of the kilim horizontally, we can see that the rectangular medallions represent simplified double-sided niches. In contrast to most examples of this type of double-sided niche medallion kilims, this one is woven in two halves and sewn together. A different interpretation of this motif can be seen on plates 61 & 64.

PUBLISHED:
Y. Petsopoulos, *Kilims,* London 1979, pl. 121. (Petsopoulos also points out the astonishing number of colours, sixteen in all.)

12
North-western Anatolia
The Galveston Collection
1.56 × 2.08 m

Relatively small and squarish kilims whose main feature is a plain red ground are a characteristic north-western Anatolian compositional type which is favoured by the Yüncü and Karakeçili tribes.

Unusually, the plain ground is enriched here by a single hexagonal hooked medallion with four protrusions terminating in small diamonds, which floats in the centre. This particular kilim was probably woven by a segment of the Yüncü tribe in the Balıkesir region. A similarly empty field and a predominantly red and blue colour scheme is found in a fragmentary piece woven in the Antalya region (plate 30).

13
North-western Anatolia
The Galveston Collection
1.32 × 2.30 m

This rare kilim must have been woven in one of the villages between Bursa and Balıkesir in north-western Anatolia. On account of its colour and structure, this kilim is the oldest one of that type known to me. The deep wedge-shaped, or finger-like, protrusions which join the red centre with the alternately blue and green field, end in short vertical lines (slits), a feature found on the central motifs of a somewhat related, but younger specimen in the Turkish and Islamic Art Museum in Istanbul (N. Ölçer, *Kilims,* Turkish and Islamic Art Museum, Istanbul 1988, pl. 12).

14
North-western Anatolia
The Galveston Collection
1.47 × 2.39 m

In concept this kilim finds parallels with plate 5, with which it shares the very wide, striped end borders and a large single medallion dominating the centre of the field. This type of kilim with long finger-like protrusions, as long as one third of the width of the piece, are only woven in some villages of the north-western corner of Anatolia, in the region between Balıkesir and Çanakkale.

15
North-western Anatolia
The Galveston Collection
0.87 × 2.22 m

The main feature of this kilim are the five main bands, each of which contains a series of five stylized hand or bird-wing motifs. This is a very rare type of kilim, of which I know only one other example in the Jack Cassin Collection.

Its colour range and various elements in its decoration suggest that it comes from the Çanakkale-Balıkesir region. The comparable piece features a rich yellow, absent from this piece, and is shorter in length (J. Cassin, *Image, Idol, Symbol, Ancient Anatolian Kelims*, New York 1989, pl. 3).

16
Central Anatolia
The Galveston Collection
0.88 × 1.52 m

This highly individual kilim was probably woven in one of the villages around the town of Karapınar. Situated halfway between Konya and Niğde, Karapınar was founded by the Ottoman government in the 16th century, and the area was populated by a number of different tribal groups of different origins, which explains why we find a variety of traditional kilim types there.

Woven against a camel-hair ground, this small kilim has a unique three-column design loosely reminiscent of the typical Yüncü composition. The tripartite motif at the top of each column is similar to the designs found in the spandrels and at the apex of the niches in the single arch 'prayer' kilims of Obruk a little further north.

17
Western Anatolia
Private Collection, New York
1.58 × 2.21 m

Woven by Koraş *yörüks* in the region between Bergama and Balıkesir, the field of this striped kilim is divided into quadrants by the subtle use of small diamonds breaking the continuity of the coloured stripes. Many related examples survive from the end of the last century (see: Ziemba, Akatay & Schwartz, *Turkish Flatweaves*, London 1979, pl. 28). However, the softness of the wool, the attention given to detail in the execution of the rather simple pattern — such as the harmonious multiple-coloured outlines to the stripes — suggest that this is perhaps the oldest surviving example of the group.

18
North-western Anatolia
Private Collection, Athens
1.73 × 2.70 m

This is one of most striking examples of a rather common type of north-western Anatolian kilim. While its composition of columns with horizontal hooked branches, and the primarily blue and red colour scheme are typical of kilims woven by segments of the Yüncü tribe in the Balıkesir region (plates 21 & 22), the addition of hooked motifs within the vertical columns and stars along the four sides, suggests it was probably woven by a Karaketçili tribal group, somewhat further south, in the Kütahya region. This is further attested by the thicker weave, and the remarkably wide range of rich colours in the infill motifs, including apricot, yellow, purple and green. Like a related, but younger piece in the Vakıflar Museum in Istanbul (B. Balpınar & U. Hirsch, 1982, pl. 47), this kilim shows that there must have been a relationship between neighbouring segments these two tribal groups.

Two comparable examples are published in: D. Black & C. Loveless, eds., *The Undiscovered Kilim*, London 1977, pl. 11; and Y. Petsopoulos, *Kilims*, London 1979, pls. 93 & 94. For Yüncü kilims see: B. Acar (Balpınar), 'Yüncü Nomad Weaving in the Balıkesir Region of Western Turkey' in *Yörük, The Nomadic Weaving of the Middle East*, A. N. Landreau ed., Pittsburgh 1978, pp. 27-31 and B. Acar (Balpınar), 'The Rugs of the Yüncü Nomads', in *HALI*, vol.2, no.2, 1979, pp. 118-120.

19
North-western Anatolia
Private Collection, New York
1.60 × 2.11 m

Few Yüncü kilims exist where the composition is built up of large hexagons within bands. A rare feature, too, is that all the plain areas were once covered in their entirety with a supplementary ornamentation of small patterns in the technique of weft-float brocading, or *zili*.

This bold yet subtle kilim was probably woven by a segment of the tribe in the Balıkesir region. It is loosely related to two much younger Yüncü kilims with a band composition. One is in the Vakıflar warehouse for carpets and kilims in Ankara (G. Erbek, Kilim Catalogue No. 1, Ankara 1988, pl. 17) and the other in a private collection (Y. Petsopoulos, *Kilims*, London 1979, pl. 90). In both pieces, however, the outer hexagons in the bands of this kilim are replaced by four hooked motifs.

20
North-western Anatolia
Private Collection, New York
1.40 × 2.19 m

This kilim with its highly unusual design is also a product of the Yüncü tribes, and was probably woven between Bursa and Balıkesir. This time, the three vertical columns, which are such a typical characteristic of Yüncü kilims, are composed of superimposed diamonds. The outer columns terminate in pairs of incurving hooks, giving them a zoomorphic appearance.

The small double-hooked motifs in mirror image, which are placed within the diamonds, are a common minor design in the decorative repertoire of Yüncü kilims (see plate 18), as are the hooked studs projecting into the field on both sides (plates 21, 22 & 26).

21 North-western Anatolia
The Galveston Collection
1.62 × 2.35 m

Another early version of the 'hooked projections from vertical columns' type of Yüncü kilims. Like plate 22, this one must also have been woven by a segment of the Yüncü tribe but probably more to the west in the Balıkesir region.

22 North-western Anatolia
The Galveston Collection
1.38 × 2.09 m

The use of a rich green characterizes early Yüncü kilims. This finely-woven piece was probably woven by a segment of the Yüncü tribe in the Kütahya region.

Although I believe in the early origin of some Anatolian kilim designs, going back to pre-Islamic times, in some cases earlier traditional meanings and Islamic values intertwine in the symbolism of kilim motifs. Here, the green central column culminates in a pointed, head-like projection, which protrudes into a dark blue panel above it. As this panel is narrower in width than its counterpart at the base of the two side columns, it gives a clear direction to the composition of this small kilim, reminiscent of a schematized Islamic prayer niche, *mihrab*.

23 North-western Anatolia
Private Collection, New York
1.71 × 2.90 m

Woven in the region around Kütahya, this kilim has a simplified variant of one of the compositions most favoured by the Yüncü (plates 21 & 22). Here, however, the central column is replaced by a series of six rectangular, denticulated medallions. The serrated, saw-tooth edges along the vertical lines and the use of double warps along the selvedges find parallels in kilims made somewhat further north, in the area between Bursa and Kelez (plates 2 & 4).

24 Western Anatolia
Private Collection, Cologne
1.82 × 3.02 m

The combination of colours in this unique kilim,

including a dark red, a dark purple, navy blue, and especially the light pink and a particularly rich yellow, are so rare in Anatolian kilims that it is difficult to give it a certain provenance, or to include it in any of the known groups. Its wool and structure are certainly Anatolian. In all probability it originates from the western parts of the country, and perhaps from Banaz, between Uşak and Afyon.

The composition is arranged in bands against a red ground, with fork-like protrusions and small comb-like motifs entering the field from the sides, in the gaps between the seven main bands. Each of these bands has at the centre a long geometric cartouche which contains four stepped diamonds framed by narrow bands. These cartouches are flanked by indented motifs, thus creating the impression that the band was split.

25 Southern Anatolia
The Galveston Collection
1.37 × 3.43 m

The field of this unpretentious kilim is divided in alternating blue and brownish-purple stripes which contain white diamonds, some of which are in natural wool, and some in cotton. The structure, the blue part of the field and the treatment of the white diamonds are features which it shares with the following pieces from the Antalya region (plates 27, 28, 29 & 30).

This piece may have been woven in the mountainous region north of Antalya, probably by the Varsak tribe who may have had a relationship to the Kazak people.

26 North-western Anatolia
Homaizi Collection, Kuwait
1.63 × 2.14 m

This striking kilim is, as far as I know, the oldest and the most unusual one of this type. It belongs to a Yüncü tribe living around the Balıkesir-Kütahya region.

The two green and tall, zoomorphic columns which flank the central blue element in the composition are reminiscent of dragons. I know only one other kilim from this group with a comparable design of zoomorphic columns, which is in the collection of Josephine Powell, and was exhibited during the Turkish Carpet Conference in Istanbul, 1984.

27 Southern Anatolia
The Galveston Collection
1.60 × 4.70 m

Until recently, very few examples were known of this distinctive group of kilims. Their main characteristics are the predominance of blue, red and white, and the use of diamond-shaped spots between hooked lozenges with pronounced stepped contours. In structure and colour these pieces share features with some other south Anatolian kilims from the Antalya region, indicating that all the kilims from this group must have been woven somewhere within the same area.

The colours and patterns of these kilims bear strong similarities to the reed screens used on the side walls of the round felt tents of the Kazak or Kırgız tribes in Central Asia, as do their long and narrow dimensions. Moreover, the emphasis on the stepped contours, which is rare in Anatolian kilims, reflects in scale the thickness of the reeds. I have, therefore, suggested an inter-relationship between these Central Asian reed screens and this group of kilims, and a similar tribal origin (B. Balpınar 'Some Anatolian Kilims and the Historical Context of their Weavers' in *Anatolian Kilims*, J. Eskenazi, ed., Milan 1984, pp. 47–48, figs. 32–36). The same attribution was subsequently also pointed out by Josephine Powell ('An Argument for the Origins of Anatolian Kilim Designs', in *Oriental Carpet & Textile Studies*, vol. 3, no. 2, p. 56, figs. 15 & 16).

This blue ground kilim has the most typical of the compositions found in this distinctive group. A related piece in the Fine Arts Museums of San Francisco has a larger pattern of diamonds within lozenges, its field colour is red and it has fewer white spots. (C. Cootner, *Anatolian Kilims, the Caroline & H. McCoy Jones Collection*, London 1990, pl. 82).

28 Southern Anatolia
The Galveston Collection
1.53 × 3.61 m

Unlike the usual composition of these kilims which consists of bands flanked by inward and outward hooks forming lozenges, as on plates 27 & 29, this one is divided into two sections by 'X' shaped hooked bands. In the spaces created at the upper and lower ends there are three rows of superimposed diamonds. As usual for this group, cotton is used for white and the field colour is blue. Two red ground kilims from this group with a similar composition are published. One is in the Turkish and Islamic Art Museum, Istanbul, (N. Ölçer, *Kilimler*, Istanbul 1989, pl. 34) and the other in the Fine Arts Museums of San Francisco (C. Cootner, *Anatolian Kilims, The Caroline & H. McCoy Jones Collection*, London 1990, pl. 83). The structure and colour of this kilim, however, suggest that it is perhaps the oldest in this group.

29 Southern Anatolia
Private Collection, Cologne
1.63 × 4.06 m

This is another piece from the Kazak-Kirgiz kilim group from the Antalya region. Like plate 27, it has two complete and two half red lozenges. Unlike it, however, the ends of the hooked bands do not extend to the end of the kilim, but terminate in a pair of hooked, head-like ends, which gives a zoomorphic impression similar to that on plate 28.

The pale green diamond in the last lozenge is cut here, probably because of the need of a certain size to surround a specific round felt tent. Another and probably younger kilim, with darker, more brownish colours which has three full and two half lozenges is published in: Eskenazi, *Anatolian Kilims*, Milan 1984, pl. 18.

30 Southern Anatolia
The Galveston Collection
1.45 × 1.85 m

This fragmentary kilim has probably lost one half of its original length. The white cotton edging on the stepped contour of the blue side borders, and along the outline of the designs, together with the colour scheme suggest that this kilim belongs to the Antalya group. Empty field red-ground kilims with blue borders are well known among the weavings of the Yüncü and Karakeçili tribes, but hitherto unknown among the Antalya kilims. Two horn-like projections come out of a column formed by diamonds flanked by two cartouches consisting of diamonds with triangular extensions. These two motifs are reminiscent of the flat, double-headed goddess figures from the Bronze Age of Anatolia and Mesopotamia.

The only other related piece is a smaller fragment in the Fine Arts Museums of San Francisco. It also shows one end of a kilim with a similar composition of a red field with a blue border and triangular corner panels (C. Cootner, *Anatolian Kilims, The Caroline & H. McCoy Jones Collection*, London 1990, pl. 101).

31 North-eastern Anatolia
The Galveston Collection
1.75 × 4.63 m

The weave and the colours of this very long kilim are typical of the Kars region in the easternmost parts of Anatolia. Despite the geographic distance, this kilim, like the previous group from Antalya, can trace its origin to reed screens. I have seen such large reed screens with similar complex multilayered designs and colours used as tent dividers in this region, and one is on display in the Archaeological and Ethnographical Museum of Kars.

The relatively narrow white borders have a series of motifs consisting of two triangles placed end to end. The same motif appears on other types of Anatolian kilims and is referred to as a *nazarlık*, an amulet to protect against the evil eye.

32 South-western Anatolia
Private Collection, Cologne
1.25 × 1.43 m

This type of small kilim with a red ground, framed by a blue border with a stepped contour, is typical of the Denizli region. The small diamonds with crosses at the centre which are scattered all over the red ground are arranged chromatically to form a pattern of diagonal lines.

33 Central Anatolia
The Galveston Collection
1.06 × 1.69 m

In this particular version of the *elibelinde* design, the doubled-up image is joined together to form a single motif. Unlike the usually pointed heads, here the heads are flattened, a feature typical of a few villages south of Sivrihisar, in the region of Eskişehir, where this piece was woven, and of some villages in the İsparta region, as plate 39. A kilim with similar end borders containing interlocked 'S' motifs is published in J. Mellaart, U. Hirsch, B. Balpınar, *The Goddess from Anatolia*, Milan 1989, vol. I, p. 68, fig. 26. One more piece with the same type of *elibelinde* motif and similar proportions is in the Vakıflar Museum in Istanbul (Balpınar & Hirsch, 1982, pl. 64).

34 South-western Anatolia
The Galveston Collection
1.45 × 2.64 m

Brightly coloured and coarsely woven kilims with a plain, red central panel flanked by wide, decorated end panels are mostly made in the region of Muğla, north of Fethiye by *yörük* tribes.

These kilims were normally woven in one piece and used as camel cloths. The plain-coloured part was placed on the back of the animal, and the decorated ends hung on its sides where they would be more visible. The end panels were variously decorated with patterns of saw-tooth-edged diamonds, hooked medallions, or *elibelinde* motifs, as in the present example.

35 South-western Anatolia
Private Collection, New York
1.08 × 4.02 m

The simplicity of this long and narrow kilim makes it difficult to give it an accurate attribution. The minimal decoration consists of lavender-purple side borders flanking a rich yellow field. The saw-tooth reciprocal outline of the field creates a continuous niche-like effect. Its colours and structure are similar to kilims woven in the region of Fethiye in southern Anatolia.

36 Central Anatolia
Georgie Wolton
1.50 × 4.35 m

The composition of this kilim is related to plates 61 & 64. It was probably woven somewhat further to the west around Haymana, south of Ankara.

When viewed horizontally, the medallions can be interpreted as double-sided niches. The rows of small hooked motifs between the large bands are similar to those in the end borders of plate 62, while the elaborate 'double-sided, double-bird' motifs at the centre of each of the large medallions, compare closely with those in the main bottom border of plate 88.
ILLUSTRATED:
D. Waterhouse, 'Orphans of the art world', *HALI*, vol.7, no.2, 1985, p. 22.

37 Central Anatolia
The Galveston Collection
1.09 × 3.55 m

Although a variety of kilims with patterns built up of *elibelinde* motifs were woven in central and south-eastern Anatolia, there is also a concentration of such kilims in western Anatolia, woven in villages whose inhabitants claim to be *yerli*, that is, native or indigenous. To cover the surface, doubled-up *elibelinde* motifs in mirror image are woven in offset rows. By arranging the colours differently, either vertically as in this piece, or, as is more common, diagonally, as in plate 33, different effects are achieved. These kilims rarely have borders. They usually have crenellated sides, and a few decorated bands as end borders. With its thick structure and strong yellow and green, this example must have been woven in one of the *yerli* villages, possibly Altınekin (Zıvrık), north of Konya.

38 South-western Anatolia
Private Collection, New York
1.40 × 3.53 m

The yellow field with a narrow saw-tooth brown edging border is decorated with a profusion of small diamonds. These are arranged chromatically to build an overall pattern of large lozenges. The bright colours, especially the strong yellow and the thick weave are typical of kilims made in the mountainous region between Fethiye and Denizli, west of Antalya, probably by a weaver related to one of the Varşak tribes.

39 South-western Anatolia
The Galveston Collection
1.50 × 2.81 m

The main bands which are separated by narrow

stripes of 'S' motifs are decorated with two different versions of the *elibelinde* design. One is a doubled-up version in mirror image, with flat heads as in plates 33, 34, 37 & 68. The other is larger, and has a skirt-like triangle topped with two 'hook' heads and a pair of incurving arms. Double-headed *elibelinde* are less common than those with a single head. This coarsely woven but colourful piece uses cotton for the white and must have been woven during one of the summer pastures in the region betweeen İsparta and Burdur by a *yörük* tribe.

40 Western Anatolia
Private Collection, Athens
1.61 × 3.66 m

The small 'spanners' scattered throughout the surface as well as the large 'X' shaped geometric medallions represent stylized animals. The juxtaposition of so many strong colours shifts the emphasis away from the pattern to create the overall effect of a patchwork. This kilim was probably woven in the Denizli area.
PUBLISHED:
Y. Petsopoulos, *From the Danube to the Euphrates, Kilims of the 18th and 19th Centuries*, Athens 1990, cat. no. 26.

41 Central Anatolia
The Galveston Collection
1.36 × 3.88 m

Kilims with a thick and heavy structure, with large, multilayered, saw-tooth edged diamonds within bands are woven in Karapınar and the surrounding villages, northeast of Konya (cf. B. Balpınar & U. Hirsch, *Flatweaves of the Vakıflar Museum, Istanbul,* Wesel 1982, pl. 6). A related fragment which has two medallions and different motifs on the wide bands is published by B. Frauenknecht, *Early Turkish Tapestries*, Nürnberg 1984, pl. 45.

42 Western Anatolia
Private Collection, New York
1.40 × 1.91 m

Kilims with a variety of motifs whose main feature are long horizontal protrusions are called by their weavers *parmaklı*, literally, with fingers. These *parmaklı* kilims are only woven in some of the *yerli* (native) villages scattered in the Eskişehir, Afyon and Kütahya regions of western Anatolia, in what was the centre of ancient Phrygia.

This is a rare type of *'parmaklı'* kilim which must have been woven in a village near Kütahya. Originally the piece must have had three panels, each containing a large multilayered medallion framed by four smaller ones. The layout of wide panels, dominated by large *parmaklı* medallions, is related to plate 48, but there the finger-like protrusions are longer and have sharper ends.

43 Western Anatolia
Victoria & Albert Museum, London,
Inv. no. 330–1894.   1.68 × 3.71 m

When this kilim, whose designs terminate in finger-like protrusions, was first published by Petsopoulos in 1979, it was left unattributed, as no information had emerged at that time about these *parmaklı* kilims. Whilst many other pieces with this composition have become known since then, this is perhaps still the earliest surviving example.

For more information about this group of kilims see: B. Balpınar & U. Hirsch, 'Parmaklı Kilims' in *HALI*, no. 26, 1985, pp. 12–17 and J. Mellaart, U. Hirsch, B. Balpınar, *The Goddess from Anatolia*, Milan 1989, vol. IV, pp. 49–54, figs. 80–90.
PUBLISHED:
Y. Petsopoulos, *Kilims*, London 1979, pl. 1.

44 Western Anatolia
Private Collection, Cologne
1.55 × 3.76 m

In structure and composition this kilim is related to the so-called *parmaklı*, 'finger-edged' kilims, especially plate 43, which originate from the Eskişehir, Afyon and Kütahya regions.

This, however, is a very rare variant of a *parmaklı* kilim, in which the protrusions are short and angular, like the vertical crenellations on plate 45. The rectilinear pattern acting as a border finds parallels with kilims woven further east, in Cappadocia (plates 87 & 89).
PUBLISHED:
P. Bausback, *Kelim, Antike Orientalische Flachgewebe*, Munich 1983, pl. 30.
H. Bartels, 'Anatolische Flachgewebe', *Kunst & Antiquitäten*, vol. 1, 1985, fig. 8.

45 Central Anatolia
The Galveston Collection
0.96 × 1.73 m

The region between Konya and Eskişehir in central Anatolia produces a variety of rugs with superimposed rectangular niches most of which are woven as *zili* (weft-float-brocaded) or *tülü* (knotted with long shaggy pile).

Tapestry-woven examples are relatively rarer, and no other is known with such an archaic rendering of these superimposed motifs, a composition which finds parallels in the façades of the rock-cut temples or tombs of the ancient Phrygians who lived in the same area (see: J. Mellaart, U. Hirsch, B. Balpınar, *The Goddess*

from Anatolia, Milan 1989, vol. IV, pp. 39–40, figs. 38–42.)

Here, because of the kilim structure, the long vertical lines which are a dominant feature of this kilim are crenellated to omit long slits, a feature that relates this piece to the three-lozenge kilim on plate 44.

46 Western Anatolia
Private Collection, Cologne
1.75 × 2.65 m

Kilims with rows of *parmaklı* medallions on a red field, woven in the *yerli-manav* villages around Eskişehir, Afyon and Kütahya are quite common, but it is very rare to find examples with good colours, such as this piece.

One of the characteristics of these kilims are the weft-float-brocaded narrow end borders, which are decorated with rows of small motifs, similar to the ones found scattered in the field.

Similar pieces are published in: B. Balpınar and U. Hirsch, *Flatweaves in the Vakıflar Museum, Istanbul*, 1982, pl. 75; C. Cootner, *Anatolian Kilims, the Caroline and H. McCoy Jones Collection*, London 1990, pl. 56; and J. Eskenazi, ed., *Anatolian Kilims*, Milan 1984, pl. 2.

47 Western Anatolia
The Galveston Collection
0.94 × 1.37 m

This colourful *parmaklı* 'prayer' kilim has a composition of superimposed niches. The effect of niches is created by a series of pointed bands interlocking with each other by means of a continuous outline of finger-like protrusions. It must have been woven in a *yerli-manav* village, literally a native village whose inhabitants grow vegetables, in the region between Afyon and Kütahya.

48 North-western Anatolia
Private Collection, New York
1.47 × 2.58 m

This kilim has a very rare version of a finger-like pattern. In general, by using curved wefts, the protrusions of *parmaklı* kilims have soft outlines and rounded ends, a decorative feature which also prevents the existence of slits. In this piece, however, the large-scale 'fingers' have a strong rectilinear quality and end sharply in diagonal lines. A chequered motif woven in weft-float brocaded, *zili* technique at the core of the central diamond, breaks the otherwise uniform pattern.

This piece must have been woven in the northern part of the region weaving *parmaklı* kilims, in one of the *yerli-manav* villages somewhere between Balıkesir, Bursa and Kütahya.

The only comparable piece I know is a fragment with two medallions, illustrated on the back cover of *HALI*, no. 38, 1988 and on the inside cover of *Gallerie Koller*, Auction 19, Zürich, March 1988.

49 Western Anatolia
The Galveston Collection
1.45 × 2.14 m

In what is a rare occurrence among traditional kilim weavers in Anatolia, the weaver of this kilim has used the traditional *parmak*, 'finger' elements to make a personal composition.

Going by its structure and the execution of 'finger' protrusions, this kilim must have been woven in the southernmost part of the *parmaklı* kilim weaving region, west of Lake Burdur in western Anatolia.

50 Central Anatolia
The Galveston Collection
1.82 × 3.50 m

This composition of this '*saff*' kilim has a strong architectural quality. The niches are arranged in groups within bands, separated from each other by a series of plain stripes. On top of the three superimposed niches with pointed arches in each band, three smaller niches are placed side-by-side, which echo conical, dome-like constructions.

'*Saff*' kilims with niches related to this one are mostly known from the Sivas region in the north-east of central Anatolia (see: Dennis Dodds, 'Anatolian Kilims from the Sivas Region', *HALI*, vol.1 no.4, 1978, pp. 319–324). However, no other example has yet come to light with this feature of multiple superimposed niches, nor with this combination of colours which are related to the previous kilim from western Anatolia (plate 48).

51 Western Anatolia
The Galveston Collection
1.36 × 3.65 m

Kilims with patterns built up of small lozenges are named in rug literature 'saw-tooth edged diamonds' or '*baklava*', after a Turkish pastry cut in the form of parallelograms. Kilims of this type are mainly woven in western Anatolia, south and east of Konya, in villages whose inhabitants claim to be '*yerli*' indigenous, or native.

Most of these large, so-called *baklava* kilims are woven in one piece on vertical looms. Examples made in two halves, such as this one, are very rare. It was probably woven in western Anatolia, in the region between Manisa and Gördes, or perhaps further north between Bursa and Eskişehir (for more information about this group see: J. Mellaart, U. Hirsch, B. Balpınar, *The Goddess from Anatolia*, Milan 1989, vol. I, p. 24, fig.5 and vol. IV, pp.54-57).

The hooked protrusions in the white band at the corners of the baklava pattern are an unusual feature, indicating that this is a white-ground kilim with an offset pattern of full and half diamond medallions. A kilim with the same pattern, but woven in one piece, is in the Vakıflar Museum in Istanbul (B. Balpınar & U. Hirsch, 1982, pl. 3).

52 .Western Anatolia
The Galveston Collection
1.88 × 3.98 m

This very fine and precisely woven kilim was probably made in the region between Manisa and Isparta in western Anatolia.

The unusual and interesting side borders are woven separately and then sewn onto the main part of the kilim. Their decoration consists of a row of small hexagonal motifs within a continuous hooked outline, which is flanked on the inside edge by a reciprocal pattern and a fingered *parmaklı* outline at the outer edge.

The central panel has three vertical rows of diamonds with hooked projections which are related to the main patterns of plates 53 & 54. The spaces between them contain two rows of rectangular, box-like motifs which are connected to each other with double-hooked diamonds similar to the ones in the vertical columns, thus creating the impression that the field is divided into a pattern of squares. As for the form of the box-like motifs, this too seems to be somehow related to the shape of the background of the kilims on plates 53 & 54.

Western Anatolia produced a variety of kilims with a similar field composition of box designs and different borders. The box form, however, appears also in kilims produced further east in a number of separate places, such as plate 96 and a piece in the Vakıflar Museum in Istanbul, which has a comparable field composition but is woven in two halves with 'vine scroll' borders and a coarser weave (B. Balpınar & U. Hirsch, 1982, pl. 24).

53 Western Anatolia
The Galveston Collection
1.50 × 2.40 m

Despite superficial differences in appearance and size, this coarse and loosely-woven kilim which must have been woven in or around Selendi, near Manisa in western Anatolia, uses the same design elements as plate 54 but on a larger scale.

The utilization of different background colours between the rows of white diamonds with hooked extensions, creates rectangular box-like

forms which are used on a variety of Anatolian kilims as separate motifs (plates 52 & 96).

The end borders contain a particular double-sided version of the *elibelinde* motif with feather-like projections on the sides which are typical of this region of western Anatolia.

54 Western Anatolia
The Galveston Collection
1.52 × 3.89 m

This kilim uses the same design vocabulary as plate 53 to create a different composition of two columns which are built up of large and small diamonds with hooked projections against a light blue ground. It must have been woven in or around Selendi in the region of Manisa in western Anatolia, and in contrast to the previous piece, it has a very fine structure akin to that of south-eastern Anatolian kilims. This relationship is further enhanced by the use of cochineal-coloured red in the centres of the small motifs. An unusual feature is the use as side borders of reciprocal projections of a type associated with Yüncü tribal kilims. The skillful matching of the small motifs on the two halves of the kilim where they are sewn together is impressive.

A visually almost indistinguishable kilim, but with a coarser structure, was exhibited by Jürg Rageth during the Basel kilim conference in 1990.

55 Western Anatolia
The Galveston Collection
1.44 × 3.76 m

The pattern of this unusual kilim is obviously derived from the designs of Yüncü tribal kilims (plates 18 & 21). Most features, however, including its long and narrow proportions, the fact that it is woven in two halves, its range of colours, and the designs of the end borders, find no parallels in Yüncü kilims.

The arrangement of colours creates a composition of concentric rectangles separated by the thin vertical columns crossed by horizontal hooked branches, so characteristic of Yüncü kilims. The effect of superimposing the hooked branches on the long sides of the rectangles creates a series of interlocking, meandering bands. The result is a unique re-interpretation of one of most common Yüncü compositions.

A fragmentary kilim with similar weave in San Francisco (C. Cootner, *Anatolian Kilims, the Caroline & H. McCoy Jones Collection*, London 1990, pl. 38) uses the outer part of the field pattern of this piece as a side border. As for the motifs in the main end borders, they appear in the dividing bands of plate 61, a kilim of similar fineness and related colouring, but woven further north between Eskişehir and Ankara.

In structure this kilim has similarities with

plate 56. They might have both been woven in the same summer pasture in the İsparta region, shared by settlements or camps of various nomadic, tribal groups.

56 Western Anatolia
Private Collection, Cologne
1.58 × 3.99 m

The separately-woven side borders of this three-part kilim are decorated with a unique continuous pattern of reciprocal hooked motifs. The midnight blue field contains three complex medallions, the central one being loosely related to the medallions on plates 57 & 58. Related medallions arranged in three pairs appear in H. Ploier, *Gewebte Poesie, Sammlung Konzett,* Graz 1991, pl. 60.

The outer medallions are much more unusual. They appear on a small number of kilims which differ from each other in colour and texture, suggesting a tribal identification with this motif by weavers living in different areas. One is a small kilim with a single medallion on a dark brown ground which was exhibited in the Douglas Hyde Gallery, Trinity College, Dublin (M. Franses and A. Marcuson, *Kilims, the Traditional Tapestries of Turkey,* Dublin 1979, cat. no. 8). Another, in the Vakıflar Museum, Istanbul has three medallions on a lighter blue ground and a different border of animal and *elibelinde* motifs (B. Balpınar & U. Hirsch, 1982, pl. 36).

This particular piece may have been woven around Lake Eğridir, in the İsparta region of western Anatolia. It is worth noting that the whirling hooked motif at the center of one of the outer medallions is a main element of some Karakeçili tribal kilims.

57 Central Anatolia
Private Collection, Cologne
1.63 × 4.06 m

This kilim and the following one must have been woven somewhere between Konya and Ankara in central Anatolia, perhaps in Sivrihisar. Related pieces, however, have been seen in Altınekin (Zvırık), somewhat further south.

Very few kilims of this distinctive design group have survived, including one in the Konzett Collection (H. Ploier, *Gewebte Poesie, Sammlung Konzett,* Graz 1991, pl. 59) and another in a private collection (J. Mellaart, U. Hirsch, B. Balpınar, *The Goddess from Anatolia,* Milan 1989, vol. I, p. 54, fig. 9), but the latter uses a different pattern to join the field to the borders. Two younger examples are published in *The world of the kilim,* Galerie Sailer, Vienna 1984, cat. no. 34, and in H. Ploier, *Gewebte Poesie, Sammlung Konzett,* Grazz 1991, pl. 58. These

two are very similar apart from distribution of a few minor motifs.

The use of cotton for the whites, navy blue for the field and red for the borders are the typical colours characteristic of this group. Kilims with medallions of a similar distinctive and complicated form, but with a thicker weave, and a different colour scheme were woven in the Torous Mountains and the İsparta-Burdur region of western Anatolia. In these kilims the medallions are set against white or red ground panels separated by narrow borders. They are still woven, largely unchanged in some *yörük* settlements in that area. (See: Josephine Powell, 'An Argument for the Origins of Anatolian Kilim Designs', in *Oriental Carpet & Textile Studies,* vol. 3, no. 2, 1989, p. 52, fig. 4, and Werner Brüggemann, 'Carpets and Kilims – a contribution to the problem of the origin of designs in Kilims', in *Oriental Carpet & Textile Studies,* vol. 3, no. 2, 1989, p. 77, fig. 13).

58 Central Anatolia
The Galveston Collection
1.68 × 4.12 m

This kilim is so similar in weave, composition and detail to the previous one that it must have been woven in the same village. The only differences between these two finely woven kilims are in the colours, where this piece has a somewhat richer quality, and in minor details, such as the scale of the small multi-hooked motifs between the main medallions, at the upper and lower ends of the field.

They demonstrate the ability of two equally skilled weavers to execute faithfully a given design, as well as the respect in which these traditional designs were held in the past.

59 North-western Anatolia
Private Collection, New York
1.58 × 2.95 m

Like plates 94, 95 & 99, the principal motif of this unique kilim is an 'X' shaped, hooked medallion, which is interpreted as a birth symbol, but its finer and flatter structure distinguishes it from the others, as does its dark blue ground.

The red border joining the blue field with a reciprocal triangular outline finds parallels in the kilims from the Balıkesir region. But the combination of this type of 'birth' symbols in the field, flanked by two end borders, one with bull-head figures in mirror image, followed by a common central Anatolian narrow reciprocal pattern, is unknown to me in western Anatolian kilims. Nevertheless, its structure and colour suggest that this kilim may originate from the region around Balıkesir.

Some of the colours and the stepped contour of the angular border seem somehow related to plate 24, another highly unusual western Anatolian kilim.

60
Central Anatolia
The Galveston Collection
1.73 × 3.74 m

This very rare kilim with very fine structure must have been woven in the region of Sivrihisar between Eskişehir and Ankara. It is woven in one piece and cotton is used to create white.

The layout consists of wide horizontal panels separated by narrow bands with interlocked 'S' motifs. The principal design element is a bird-like form. These 'birds' are paired tail-to-tail at the ends of the panels, and the pairs are doubled-up in mirror image at the centre. The spaces between the 'birds' form large hooked medallions which contain a two-layered motif with a denticulated outline.

Half of a two-part kilim with similar medallions, but with entirely different colours and texture was published in B. Frauenknecht, *Early Turkish Tapestries*, Nürnberg 1984, pl. 19. However, because the sides are framed with a reciprocal pattern and the main motifs are filled with small hooked ornaments, the composition lacks the clarity of this piece and cannot be easily understood.

61
Central Anatolia
The Galveston Collection
1.50 × 4.01 m

Probably woven in the Sivrihisar region, southwest of Ankara.

When the kilim is viewed horizontally, we find that the main element of the decoration is a condensed version of the double-sided niche motif found on plates 3, 4, 7, 8 & 11. The juxtaposition of these double-sided niches creates the impression of a kilim with bands of saw-tooth edged medallions, a compositional feature shared by plates 36, 62 & 64, except that here each band contains three medallions instead of the usual two.

A piece with the same composition but with incredibly rich, saturated colours and cotton white is published in Y. Petsopoulos, *From the Danube to the Euphrates, Kilims of the 18th and 19th Centuries*, Athens 1990, cat. no. 31. The brightness of its colours may be explained by its having been kept in a chest (*sandık*) for generations, used only on special occasions. Nevertheless, the colours of the piece illustrated here look older, not only because of use, but because of age.

Another comparable piece is published in H. Ploier, *Gewebte Poesie, Sammlung Konzett*, Graz 1991, pl. 37.

62
Central Anatolia
Private Collection, Cologne
1.55 × 4.09 m

Like the previous piece, this kilim must have been woven in one of the villages in the region between Ankara and Eskişehir. While belonging to the same compositional type, the rectangular, squarish shape of the double-sided niches give this piece a highly individual look.

As is the case with most of the older traditional kilims, we have no means of dating this piece. However, its pinkish red, light green and blue are colours associated with early Anatolian pile carpets.
PUBLISHED:
J. Mellaart, U. Hirsch, B. Balpınar, *The Goddess from Anatolia*, Milan 1989, vol. I, p. 82, fig. 6 (detail).

63
Central Anatolia
The Galveston Collection
1.45 × 3.00 m

This finely-woven kilim must have been woven around Aksaray, northeast of Konya in central Anatolia. When viewed horizontally, the larger panels divided by ornamented bands are seen clearly as double-sided pointed niches similar to those on plates 9 & 10.

This kilim which is woven in one piece demonstrates perfectly the principle of the mirror image along the horizontal axis, not as a means of matching two halves of a kilim, but as a decorative statement.

The basic motif inside each niche, which consists of a small saw-tooth edged diamond medallion with two pairs of hooked extensions on either side, is doubled-up reflecting the mirroring of the niche forms.

A closely related piece with an identical composition is published in J. Mellaart, U. Hirsch, B. Balpınar, *The Goddess from Anatolia*, Milan 1989, vol. I, p. 81, fig. 3, and another, which is woven in two halves and has two wide end-borders, in B. Frauenknecht, *Early Turkish Tapestries*, Nürnberg 1984, pl. 39. A third related kilim in the Fine Arts Museums of San Francisco (C. Cootner, *Anatolian Kilims, the Caroline & H. McCoy Jones Collection*, London 1990, pl. 16) is also woven in two parts, with two extra end-borders. Its niches are broader and it has different designs in the dividing bands.

64
Central Anatolia
Private Collection, New York
1.45 × 2.70 m

The identical use of narrow polychrome stripes dividing the main bands and the total coincidence of the colours indicate that this fragmentary kilim, which is missing part of the last panel and the end border, must have been woven in the same village as plate 63.

These two closely related pieces have a different composition, thus demonstrating the variety of designs used by a single group of weavers. The saw-tooth edged diamonds here are of the same type as those on plate 61, while the composition is similar to plate 36, but there the colours and the dividing bands are very different.

65 Western Anatolia
The Galveston Collection
1.73 × 4.60 m

I believe that this very finely woven kilim is an elaboration of an ancient form by Türkmen weavers who wove for the market.

The 'X'-like medallions with four pairs of long hooked 'arms', sprouting from a small hexagonal body are an exaggerated version of the typical Türkmen kilim medallions found on plate 76. The border designs at the sides and the ends can be seen on many other types of Türkmen kilims woven in several places in Anatolia. The reciprocal motif joining the borders to the field is made up by a series of little figures.

The colours and the texture of this particular example suggest it was woven in western Anatolia between Aydın and Denizli. It is woven in two halves and sewn together perfectly. A piece with the same field and border decoration is published in B. Frauenknecht, *Anatolian Kilims*, Nürnberg 1982, pl. 16, while another, with different side borders and woven in three parts was published in Y. Petsopoulos, *Kilims*, London 1979, pl. 147, and in D. Black & C. Loveless, eds. *The Undiscovered Kilim*, London 1977, pl. 16.

66 Western Anatolia
The Galveston Collection
1.16 × 3.47 m

The small stepped diamonds covering the entire surface of this kilim give it a mosaic-like appearance. The colours are arranged to form a pattern of three large lozenges. Because of its colour and structure this kilim may have been woven in the Denizli-Aydın region.

Similar stepped diamonds appear on one of the early archaeological finds which can be defined as a 'kilim' which was discovered in Gordion near Ankara, dating from 700 B.C. (see: L. Bellinger 'Textiles from Gordion', in *The Bulletin of the Needle and Bobbin Club*, 1962, pp. 4-33; B. Balpınar & U. Hirsch, *Flatweaves of the Vakıflar Museum, Istanbul*, Wesel 1982, p. 21, note 20; and J. Mellaart, U. Hirsch, B. Balpınar, *The Goddess from Anatolia*, Milan 1989, vol. III, pp. 59, 60 & 101).

PUBLISHED:
H. Bartels, 'Anatolische Flachgewebe', *Kunst & Antiquitäten*, vol. 1, 1985, fig. 1.

67 Central Anatolia
The Galveston Collection
1.41 × 4.42 m

This kilim was woven by one of the Türkmen tribes in the Konya-Aksaray region. The white central field is framed on all four sides by red reciprocal stepped triangles. It contains large hexagonal medallions with protrusions derived from 'carnation' or 'goddess with birds' motifs on the two flat sides, and traditional *elibelinde* figures at the apex of each side.

The end panels which are decorated with a pattern of so-called *gülbudak*, double bird motifs, are so large as to seem part of another kilim. They terminate in narrow white bands with a row of motifs named by weavers 'sitting dogs', indicating the zoomorphic origin of the design.
PUBLISHED:
Y. Petsopoulos, *Kilims*, London 1979, pl. 153.
H. Bartels, 'Anatolische Flachgewebe', *Kunst & Antiquitäten*, vol. 1, 1985.
H. Bartels, 'Connoisseur's Choice', *HALI*, 1987, issue 36, pp. 16-17.

68 Central Anatolia
Private Collection, New York
1.22 × 3.96 m

The most commonly used form of the *elibelinde* design, as an overall field ornament, is the doubled-up version in mirror image, which produces a diamond shaped motif. Depending on how the colours of these diamonds are arranged, different patterns emerge.

In western Anatolian native, *yerli*, villages it is mostly used on kilims without side borders and the colours of the motifs are arranged vertically or diagonally. However, a variety of kilims with *elibelinde* motifs are also woven by various Türkmen tribal segments settled between these villages as well as further east.

The Türkmen arrange the colours of the motifs in diamonds, as in this piece, which was woven by one of these Türkmen tribes settled between Niğde and Aksaray. Kilims with a related pattern and colours have also been found further north, in the region between Sivas and Tokat. As usual for a Türkmen kilim, this one must have had side borders and some more end borders, which would have given it a more crowded look.
PUBLISHED:
J. Mellaart, U. Hirsch, B. Balpınar, *The Goddess from Anatolia*, Milan 1989, vol. I, p. 66, fig. 21.

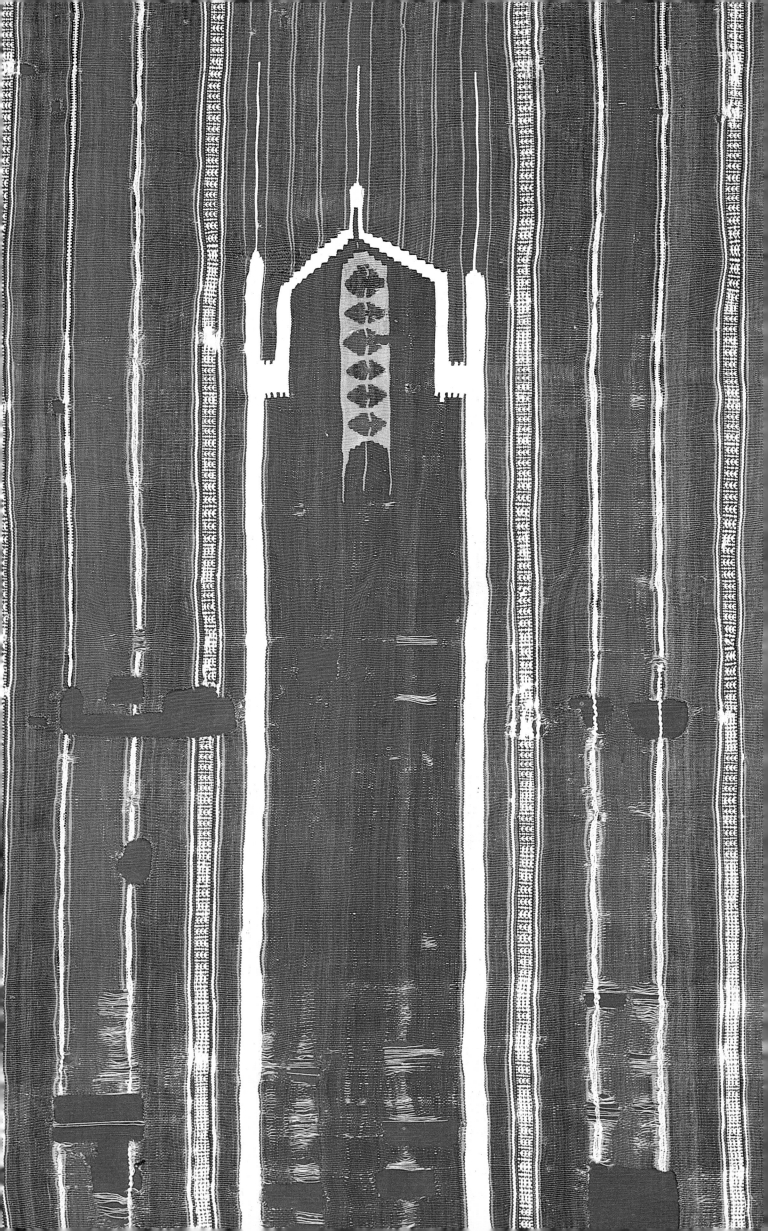

69

Eastern Anatolia
Private Collection, New York
0.76 × 3.76 m

Among the kilim designs of Anatolia there is one which is used almost everywhere, a figure which sometimes appears as a complete motif and sometimes as part of a motif. It has a head-like form with two incurving hooks on two sides. The weavers consider it to be a female symbol and call it *elibelinde*, literally, hands-on-hips.

The *elibelinde* figure is the main motif of this kilim. But the spike-edged extensions to the *elibelinde*, with two stick-like studs at the base, may be interpreted as birds.

The depiction of female goddesses with two birds is known from the Neolithic period up to the Roman era, and although there is still much debate and discussion about the iconography of this motif, I, along with many other authors on Anatolian kilims, interpret the *elibelinde* as an important female, the 'Goddess', with two stylized birds.

The most common use of the *elibelinde* in Anatolian kilims is with its form doubled-up in mirror image, as it appears on plates 33, 37 & 68. Here, however, in line with the original idea of the Goddess with two birds, single versions of the *elibelinde* motifs are placed in alternate bands. They are only doubled-up in the central panel.

This panel must be the other half of the one in the Fine Arts Museums of San Francisco (C. Cootner, *Anatolian Kilims, the Caroline & H. McCoy Jones Collection*, London 1990, pl. 78). I do not know another similar piece, but its structure and colour suggest it may have been woven somewhere south of Sivas in eastern Anatolia.

70

Central Anatolia
The Galveston Collection
0.69 × 3.69 m

This very fine half of a kilim must have been woven in the region between Aksaray and Niğde. Cotton as well as natural wool are used to create a contrast between a bright white and a cream white.

No direct parallel can be found for this piece. A related field pattern appears on two kilims with a more geometric character, and woven in a different region. One is in the Vakıflar Kilim Museum in Istanbul (B. Balpınar & U. Hirsch, 1982, pl. 41) and the other is published in B. Frauenknecht, *Anatolian Kilims*, Nürnberg 1982, pl. 9.

In both these kilims, the continuous row of hexagons which makes up the field pattern of this piece, has been broken up into medallions. Moreover, unlike these two comparisons, where continuous repeat borders unrelated to the field pattern are used, here the border design is directly related to that of the field.

71

Central Anatolia
The Galveston Collection
1.50 × 4.15 m

Woven somewhere around Ankara in central Anatolia, this kilim was made in two halves which joined very well when they were sewn together.

When viewed horizontally, hexagons with double-hooked projections (the *elibelinde* 'goddess' forms) are attached to each other, like plate 82, and even more so plate 78. Between these *elibelinde* forms there are smaller projections, again with a hexagonal body form and two incurving arms with a head in between. The double bird-like feathered motifs on both the end borders are interesting. They look like symmetrical variants of the zoomorphic end-border motif on plate 73.

In some other places the same design is woven in one piece such as a kilim in the Vakıflar Museum in Istanbul (B. Balpınar & U. Hirsch, 1982, pl. 37), or with separate borders (J. Cassin, *Image, Idol, Symbol, Ancient Anatolian Kelims*, New York 1989, pl. 8). Sometimes one hexagon and its extensions are used as a separate medallion (J. Mellaart, U. Hirsch, B. Balpınar, *The Goddess from Anatolia*, Milan 1989, vol. I, p. 55, pls. 10 & 11).

72

Central Anatolia
The Galveston Collection
1.40 × 4.10 m

An exceptionally rare feature of this kilim which is woven in one piece, is that it only has a border on one of its long sides. It is probable that it originally had a second side border, which was woven separately.

Its large medallions are related to the continuous row of hexagons in the field of plate 70. Here, however, the design is on a larger scale and broken up into pairs of hexagons with projections to cover the entire width of the field.

This kilim may have been woven in the region between Niğde and Ankara. I do not know any other piece similar to this, which seems to be a personal interpretation of a design by an individual weaver.

73

Central Anatolia
The Galveston Collection
1.50 × 3.66 m

This fragmentary two-part kilim must come from one of the villages between Niğde and Nevşehir in ancient Cappadocia. The rectangular box-like motifs are loosely related to the ones on plates 52 & 53, and more directly to those on plate 96. Here, they are more elongated, and have a pronounced crenellated outline on the vertical sides of the motifs.

Instead of borders, the long sides are framed

by a red saw-tooth design with stick-like projections, which forms a reciprocal pattern as it joins the field. The design of the end borders is very rare. Inside zig-zag bands, there are interesting motifs of a distinct zoomorphic character with curved hooks on one side.

There is one half of a kilim with very similar 'box' forms, but with different side and end borders in the Fine Arts Museums of San Francisco (C. Cootner, *Anatolian Kilims, the Caroline & H. McCoy Jones Collection,* London 1990, pl. 64).

74
Central Anatolia
Private Collection, New York
1.50 × 3.70 m

This piece, which belongs to the group of tripartite medallion kilims, is woven in one piece, probably in one of the native, *yerli*, villages in the Nevşehir region of ancient Cappadocia. It uses red as a ground colour which is very rare in this striking group of kilims.

The drawing of the medallions seems to be simpler, without the many decorative elements of other examples in this group (plate 75). The side frames with diamonds attached to each other are related to a piece published in J. Cassin, *Image, Idol, Symbol, Ancient Anatolian Kelims*, New York 1989, pl. 2.

75
Central Anatolia
Private Collection, Cologne
1.88 × 4.24 m

This kilim may have been woven by a Türkmen tribe around Konya and Aksaray. It is woven in two halves and shares with the next piece (plate 76) a very common set of borders which is used on many types of kilims associated with the Türkmen.

The principal design of this kilim is a distinctive tripartite medallion. It is used in kilims from different parts of Anatolia with several variations in the details. But the main form is a hexagonal body and two heads. Sometimes the heads have indentations (plate 74) while others, as in this case, are pointed and decorated with hooks and the *elibelinde* symbol. The idea of this form may have derived from the flat figurines which are believed to represent the Bronze age goddesses from Mesopotamia and Anatolia.

There are relatively few such tripartite medallion kilims, a fact that is concealed by the number of published examples. There are two in the Fine Arts Museums of San Francisco (C. Cootner, *Anatolian Kilims, The Caroline & H. McCoy Jones Collection*, London 1990, pls. 75 & 76). Two more are in the Vakıflar Museum in Istanbul (B. Balpınar & U. Hirsch, 1982, pl. 32; and J. Mellaart, U. Hirsch, B. Balpınar, *The*

Goddess from Anatolia, Milan 1989, vol. I, p. 102, fig. 3), and two striking halves in the collection of Jack Cassin (J. Cassin, *Image, Idol, Symbol, Ancient Anatolian Kelims*, New York 1989, pls. 1 & 2). One is published in J. Eskenazi, ed., *Anatolian Kilims*, Milan 1984, pl. 13; and another in B. Frauenknecht, *Anatolian Kilims*, Nürnberg 1982, pl. 8.

The differences in colour, structure and interpretation of the same design elements in all these kilims show how certain designs can be carried by nomadic Türkmen weavers to different places and woven with the borders of other kilim types.

PUBLISHED:
Y. Petsopoulos, *Kilims*, London 1979, pl. 142
HALI, vol. 2, no. 4, p. 332.

76
Central Anatolia
The Galveston Collection
1.68 × 3.86 m

This type of white-ground kilim with large hooked medallions is identified as the product of Türkmen weavers. Variations of this theme are produced in many parts of Anatolia. This example must have been woven by one of the Türkmen tribal groups (probably Hotamış Türkmen) east of Konya.

It is woven in two halves and contains one of the typical versions of the hexagonal medallion with several hooked projections. Unlike plate 71 where the hexagons are joined together, here they are used as separate units with hooked extensions on the sides.

In one of the end borders, so-called carnation, or goddess-with-vultures, motifs are used. On the side borders, symmetric floral motifs are placed in compartments. The layout and decoration of the borders compares closely with another Türkmen kilim with a different centre, plate 75.

A very similar kilim is published in J. Rageth, *Kilim, Primitive Symbols of Mythology*, Rome 1986, pl. 16; another in B. Frauenknecht, *Anatolian Kilims*, Nürnberg 1982, pl. 17, and a third, from the Sivas region, in J. Mellaart, U. Hirsch, B. Balpınar, *The Goddess from Anatolia*, Milan 1989, vol. I, p. 47, fig. 4. A kilim with the same field design, same side and outer end borders but woven in one piece is in the Vakıflar Museum of Istanbul (B. Balpınar & U. Hirsch, 1982, pl. 38).

77
Central Anatolia
Private Collection, Cologne
1.78 × 3.61 m

The upper and lower parts of the unusual large motifs, which are arranged in rows on the main field of this kilim are related to the so-called 'carnation' motif.

There are comparable but clearly directional

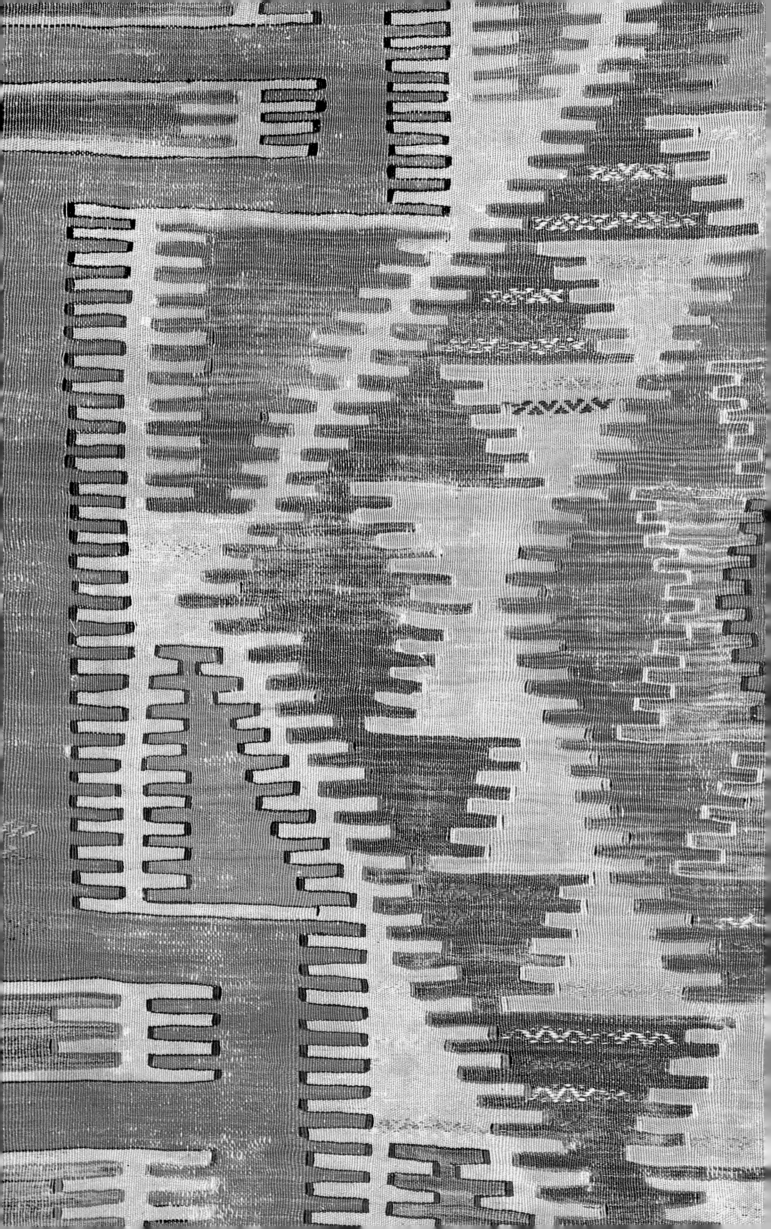

variations of this motif on two kilim fragments, one in the Fine Arts Museums of San Francisco (C. Cootner, *Anatolian Kilims, the Caroline & H. McCoy Jones Collection*, London 1990, pl. 62), and the other in a private collection (J. Mellaart, U. Hirsch, B. Balpınar, *The Goddess from Anatolia*, Milan 1989, vol. I, p. 63, fig. 12).

Perhaps more relevantly, a simplified, and more regularly symmetrical version of this motif appears on two other kilims, the first in the Vakıflar Museum in Istanbul (B. Balpınar & U. Hirsch, 1982, pl. 26) and the other published in B. Frauenknecht, *Early Turkish Tapestries*, Nürnberg 1984, pl. 6. On both these pieces the central part of the motif is shaped like a feathered rectangle, while here it appears as a triangle-edged hexagon. The connection with the Frauenknecht piece is further strengthened by its main border motif which appears within cartouches in the end borders of this piece, as well as by its structure. In colours and details, however, it compares best with the fragment in J. Mellaart, U. Hirsch, B. Balpınar, *The Goddess from Anatolia*, Milan 1989, vol. I, p. 63, fig. 12.

The tripartite motif forming a reciprocal pattern with the field on the sides of the field is an interesting and rare feature of this piece, as are the 'X' shaped motifs with a two-coloured, striped interior on the side borders (a simplified version without the striped interior appears in C. Cootner, *Anatolian Kilims, The Caroline & H. McCoy Jones Collection*, London 1990, pl. 89).

Despite relationships in design between all these pieces, there are differences in colours and structure, indicating different origins. This one must have been woven in the region between Eskişehir and Ankara, perhaps in Mihalıççık.
PUBLISHED:
M. Volkmann, ed., *Old Eastern Carpets, Masterpieces in German Private Collections*, Munich 1985, pl. 42.

78 Western Anatolia
The Galveston Collection
0.90 × 3.25 m

This piece, which must have been woven in the İsparta region, seems to be the central panel of a kilim of which the side borders were woven separately. It is a different interpretation of the same composition as plate 71.

From the sides of the hexagons which are arranged in a continuous row along the vertical axis extend pairs of *elibelinde*-like incurving hooks. However, because the head forms are missing, these extensions can also be considered as 'rams'-horns' motifs. The row of hexagons terminates on both ends of the field in a pair of hooks with crenellated necks.

The different field colours between the pairs of hooks flanking the hexagons, contain small one-directional anthropomorphic motifs with open hands and legs. In the large end panels, two long toothed lines projecting from the central four hooks end in bird-like forms.

79 Central Anatolia
The Galveston Collection
1.58 × 3.50 m

This kilim was probably woven by one of the Türkmen tribes in the Aksaray region. Hexagonal medallions built up of layers of reciprocal hooks around a saw-tooth-edged diamond centre, are widely used as central elements in a variety of kilim compositions. In this case, the field contains a row of four large medallions, the spaces between which are filled with smaller versions of the same type.

The elaborate reciprocal pattern at the edge of the white field helps to prevent the existence of long slits on the vertical sides of the kilim. A younger kilim with similar medallions was published in Y. Petsopoulos, *Kilims*, London 1979, pl. 141. A closer comparison can be made with a half kilim published in H. Ploier, *Gewebte Poesie, Sammlung Konzett*, Graz 1991, pl. 52, which aside from the similarities of pattern is also related in terms of colour and weave.

80 Central Anatolia
Private Collection, Cologne
1.78 × 4.07 m

This type of hexagonal medallion surrounded by small diamonds may owe its origin to Sassanian and Byzantine textiles with circular medallions and little pearl-like circles around. These medallions, usually in two rows, are a common design of Türkmen tribes to the east of Konya. Separately woven side borders and multiple end borders are also a very common custom of Türkmen weavers.

This kilim with a single row of medallions on blue ground must have been woven by one of these tribes, between Konya and Aksaray. The bird-like forms with reciprocal multihooks in the spaces between the medallions are very rare.

81 Western Anatolia
The Galveston Collection
1.55 × 3.55 m

Few white-ground kilims with this general type of border layout are known, and they all seem to be of considerable age. A black zig-zag band with a saw-tooth-edged baklava outline separates the white field from the plain red border, and forms a pattern of reciprocal triangles.

This compositional characteristic appears on

two more white-ground kilims. One is published in C. Cootner, *Anatolian Kilims, The Caroline & H. McCoy Jones Collection*, London 1990, pl. 40; and the other in B. Balpınar & U. Hirsch, 1982, pl. 39. Like this piece, they have two rows of medallions, flanked at the ends by a series of bands. But while the layout is the same, the motifs used are different, as is their structure.

The hexagonal medallions in the field of this kilim have four inward-hooking projections akin to 'bird heads' with small horizontal tuft-like studs. The *elibelinde* figure in the outer end borders is of the single 'goddess' type, in contrast to the twin 'goddess' variety on plates 9 & 39. This kilim may have been woven by one of the *yörük* tribes in the Manisa region of west Anatolia.

82
Central Anatolia
The Galveston Collection
0.84 × 3.07 m

The colour and structure of this fragmentary half of a kilim with the end border missing, suggest that it must have been woven somewhere in the Nevşehir region in ancient Cappadocia.

When viewed horizontally, a blue band forms a series of niche-like forms. One of the many variants of the *elibelinde*, 'hands-on-hips' motif is placed at the apex of each 'niche', and its head-like form is repeated inside the 'niche'.

Though still highly controversial, there is a general tendency to accept the idea that this type of motif, consisting of a head-like form with two incurving hooked arms, represents the fertility-mother goddesses of Near Eastern pre-history, whose cults, with variations and under different names, continued up to the Christian era. (See: J. Mellaart, U. Hirsch, B. Balpınar, *The Goddess from Anatolia*, Milan 1989; C. Cootner, *Anatolian Kilims, the Caroline & H. McCoy Jones Collection*, London 1990; B. Balpınar, 'A Discussion on Central Asian Türkmen Influence on Anatolian Kilims', in *Oriental Carpet and Textile Studies*, vol. 3, no. 2, 1989, pp. 7–17.)

The use of saw-tooth-edged, *baklava* patterned diamonds in and out of such niche-like forms, is very rare. A related kilim in two halves can be seen in Y. Petsopoulos, *Kilims*, London 1979, pl. 136, although the execution of the pattern differs because of different weaves. Petsopoulos, however, shows next to it (pl. 137) a complete piece which is almost identical to this one in both detail and execution, and shows that when the two halves are joined together the niches form hexagonal medallions.

83
Central Anatolia
The Galveston Collection
1.49 × 3.73 m

This white-ground kilim belongs to a small group

whose composition is based on denticulated diamond medallions floating on a uniform ground which is framed by a plain border forming a triangular outline as it merges with the field. These kilims have large, skirt-like end borders, and while they are mostly known to be woven in the Sivas region, there are some woven around Karapınar, near Konya.

Usually, the denticulated diamonds are placed in a lozenge formation, but here the colours are arranged to form a 'V' shaped, or 'niche' pattern. In the wide end-borders we find different arrangements of the same medallions on a smaller scale set against a black ground; at the lower end, the diamonds form diagonal bands, while at the top end, they again form a 'V' shaped or 'niche' pattern.

84
Eastern Anatolia
Private Collection, New York
1.63 × 4.32 m

This kilim, woven on a rich apricot ground, has a composition similar to the previous one. The denticulated medallions are again arranged in the shape of a 'V' or niche. In the wide end-borders the same medallions are placed in horizontal bands between narrow stripes with diagonal bands. This piece must have been woven in the Sivas region of eastern Anatolia.

Not many kilims from this group are published. One such piece with a similar orange ground appeared in B. Frauenknecht, *Early Turkish Tapestries*, Nürnberg 1984, pl. 44.

85
Eastern Anatolia
Galveston Collection
1.60 × 3.84 m

Although kilims with multiple niches in horizontal rows are considered to be woven for Islamic prayer, each niche for one person, the idea of the single niche, multiple niches, or arcades already existed as a sacred symbol in pre-Islamic religions.

The form of the niches in this type of '*saff*' kilims cannot be compared to the *mihrab*, the prayer niche of mosques which were said to have influenced the origin of the niche on prayer kilims. Neither do they represent an arcade. They seem instead to represent the head and body of a human being, or an Anatolian tombstone whose shape is equally anthropomorphic. This particular example is probably from Şarkışla, south of Sivas. A fragmentary kilim with the same type of niches which is perhaps younger is published in H. Ploier, *Gewebte Poesie, Sammlung Konzett*, Graz 1991, pl. 80.

(For information on multiple arch, *saff* kilims, see: D. Dodds, 'Anatolian kilims from the Sivas region', in *HALI*, vol. I, no. 4, 1978, pp. 319–324; B. Balpınar, 'Anatolian Kilims, Past and Present', in J. Mellaart, U. Hirsch, B. Balpınar, *The*

Goddess from Anatolia, Milan 1990, vol. IV, pp. 33–41; W. Denny, 'Saff and Sejjadeh, Origins and Meaning of the Prayer Rug', in *Oriental Carpet Studies*, vol. 3, no. 2, 1989, pp. 93–104.)

86
Central Anatolia
Private Collection, Cologne
1.42 × 3.77 m

This kilim may have been woven in Sille, a town very near Konya. When viewed horizontally, saw-tooth edged triangles, connected by crenellated bands, form a series of niches or an arcade. Large and small hooked motifs decorate the inside and outside of these double-ended niches.

The same field design appears in a kilim in the Fine Arts Museums of San Francisco (C. Cootner, *Anatolian Kilims, The Caroline & H. McCoy Jones Collection*, London 1990, pl. 11). That piece, however, is entirely free of infill motifs, and its end borders have different versions of the motifs used here.

87
Central Anatolia
The Galveston Collection
1.67 × 4.26 m

This large kilim with a strict geometric character may have been woven in the Niğde-Nevşehir region of central Anatolia. The composition consists of five panels filled with two rows of large comb-like designs with crenellated edges, and is very similar to plate 89. The same comb-like motifs are sometimes used in kilims woven with a plain camel wool field. The double bull's-head, hooked motifs in the field and along the end borders are found on many Cappadocian kilims (plates 74, 91, 92 & 93).

A kilim with a similar composition but with no infill motifs in the main panels is published in H. Ploier, *Gewebte Poesie, Sammlung Konzett*, Graz 1991, pl. 65.

88
Western Anatolia
The Galveston Collection
1.57 × 3.88 m

Although this kilim has a very free look, and displays great individual creativity, in reality only traditional, symbolic motifs are used. It was probably woven by a free-handed weaver in the region around İsparta, in western Anatolia, who could balance every empty space with motifs from her traditional repertoire.

After several end borders, she began with the idea of arranging the field in bands, containing a hexagon with double incurving hooked projections like plate 78. She then divided the central hexagon in two, and proceeded to fill the spaces between them with other hexagons. In the process, the initial concept of bands was lost, and a patchwork effect was created.

As both the field and border designs are on a brown ground, she used a continuous red saw-tooth pattern, edged in yellow to act as a divider between them. However, the unevenness of the central decoration meant that this could not be woven properly, and the irregular result adds to the 'free' look of the kilim.

89
Central Anatolia, Cappadocia
Private Collection, Athens
1.57 × 4.07 m

Stark, simple geometry combined with well balanced colours, notable among them a strong yellow and a light, lavender mauve, characterize this type of kilim woven in the Cappadocian villages.

While the composition and the large comb-like, rectangular motifs of this kilim are identical to plate 87, all the minor designs in the panels and the borders are different. Of note too, are the narrow weft-float brocaded bands framing the panels which are absent on plate 87.
PUBLISHED:
Y. Petsopoulos, *From the Danube to the Euphrates, Kilims of the 18th and 19th Centuries*, Athens 1990, cat. no. 32.

90
Central Anatolia
The Galveston Collection
1.45 × 3.20 m

This simple band kilim is woven in two halves. The principal element in its decoration are symmetrical head-like forms in bands, separated by plain purple-brown coloured bands. Its colour and structure indicate that it was probably woven in the region around Nevşehir, in ancient Cappadocia. The unusual motif in the end borders also appears on plates 89 & 91, which come from the same area.

91
Central Anatolia
The Galveston Collection
1.44 × 1.70 m

This colourful small kilim must have been woven between Niğde and Nevşehir. It is decorated with a version of the saw-tooth-edged diamond pattern, known as *baklava*.

Many groups of weavers from many different areas use this pattern (plates 51 & 92), but each gives it a clearly distinct character. Here, the *baklava* pattern is set between white bands, and forms two large medallions on a red ground. The use of the motif in the bands is widespread in Anatolia, and it is often used on a larger scale as a field design.

92
Central Anatolia
Private Collection, Cologne
1.71 × 3.67 m

Saw-tooth edged diamond, *baklava* patterns in bands in a number of compositional variations are mostly seen in kilims woven southeast and east of Konya. This one, with its typical yellow and green, must have been woven in one of the so-called *yerli* 'native' villages near Ürgüp in ancient Cappadocia, where similar kilims are woven to this day.

The predominance of yellow and the almost complete absence of white is without parallel in other groups of Anatolian kilims.

PUBLISHED:
J. Rageth, ed., *Anatolische Kelims, Symposium Basel, die Vorträge*, Basel 1990, p. 19.

93
Central Anatolia
Private Collection, New York
1.37 × 3.50 m

This design of this kilim is very similar to the previous piece (plate 92). Here the saw-tooth edged pattern is drawn on a larger scale and divided into five panels, whereas the other had six. It must have been woven in the same village near Ürgüp in ancient Cappadocia. Unlike the previous piece, which was in two halves, this one is woven as a single piece, and the end borders with double bull's-head motifs are set against a white background.

94
Central Anatolia
Private Collection, New York
1.15 × 2.09 m

The main motif of this unique small kilim is considered by some to be an ancient 'birth' symbol. It is taken to represent the goddess in the birth-giving position, legs pointing upward and arms and hands pointing down. For the iconography of this motif, see M. Allen, *The Birth Symbol in Traditional Woman's Art from Eurasia and the Western Pacific*, Toronto Museum of Textiles, 1981; and J. Mellaart, U. Hirsch, B. Balpınar, *The Goddess from Anatolia*, Milan 1989, vol. IV, pp. 41–45.

I believe this kilim may have been woven in one of the *yerli* 'native' villages in the Sivas region, as the crenellated reciprocal side pattern is used mainly in kilims from that area. A very rare feature of this piece are the two vertical stripes built up by triangles which flank the central row of motifs. As far as I know, there is no kilim comparable to this, either in a collection or in publication.

PUBLISHED:
J. Mellaart, U. Hirsch, B. Balpınar, *The Goddess from Anatolia*, Milan 1989, vol. I, p. 49, fig. 5.

95
Central Anatolia
Private Collection, New York
1.57 × 3.49 m

The series of long and short denticulated rectangular bands on both sides of this piece, which form a reciprocal pattern with the field, is a typical feature of kilims from the Sivas region, where this kilim was probably woven. The same geometric concept is used on two kilims from Cappadocia, plates 87 & 89, as the main element of their decoration.

The eight 'X' shaped 'birth' symbols on the plain red ground are similar to those found on plates 94 & 99. The wide end panels have a series of well-drawn borders including bands of *elibelinde* motifs and bull's-head symbols in mirror image. The use of six-pointed stars within hexagons in the narrow borders is rare.

96
South-eastern Anatolia
The Galveston Collection
1.50 × 4.80 m

This kilim with a unique composition was probably woven in the Maraş region in southeast Anatolia.

At first sight it looks like an ordinary band kilim. The large main bands which are separated by narrow bands of interlocked 'S' motifs contain two rows of saw-tooth edged diamonds. But the addition of small 'niche' forms of the most common variety, to both sides of the large bands, turns this piece into a rare type of 'double-sided niche', *saff* kilim.

97
Central Anatolia
The Galveston Collection
1.74 × 4.66 m

This is another variation of the so-called 'box' motif (plates 52, 53 & 54). Here the box-like rectangular forms are enlarged to cover the whole width of the field. This kilim has separately-woven borders with an unusual pattern of reciprocal stepped niche-like triangles. Similar pieces can be seen in a number of *yerli* villages in different parts of Cappadocia, such as Gelveri, near Niğde.

A very similar border pattern is used on another long three-part kilim (*The world of the kilim*, Galerie Sailer, Vienna 1984, cat. no. 35). In weave and colours, however, the two pieces have no relationship.

A half kilim published in H. Ploier, *Gewebte Poesie, Sammlung Konzett*, Graz 1991, pl. 41 has related box-like medallions, the outlines of which are also related to the medallions of plate 73.

98
Central Anatolia
The Galveston Collection
1.61 × 3.70 m

The field motifs of this kilim, which are floral in appearance, are named by most weavers *gülbudak*, rose branches, but in some villages on the Torous mountains the same motif is referred to as *saksağan*, a magpie.

Like the *elibelinde,* the *gülbudak* is one of the most widespread motifs in Anatolian kilims. Their wide distribution and great number of variations attest to their being among the oldest kilim designs.

The red and white reciprocal side ends are unusual in such a banded kilim, while the end borders have a row of motifs usually associated with Türkmen tribal kilims (plates 65 & 79). This kilim must have been woven in one of the villages in the the Yozgat-Tokat region in the northern parts of Central Anatolia.

99
Central Anatolia
Private Collection, New York
1.43 × 3.17 m

This is another rare kilim with 'birth' symbols in the shape of four-hooked 'X' shaped motifs. Although these motifs are quite common in Anatolian and Caucasian kilims, I do not know of any other with this combination of colours and designs.

A number of the minor infill ornaments, including six-pointed stars, at the centre of the main hooked motifs and in the spaces between them, are known from kilims woven in the southeastern parts of Anatolia, and around Aleppo.

The unusual reciprocal pattern edging the sides, the double-hooked triangular motifs in the end borders, as well as the colouring, suggest that this piece may have been woven in the region between Maraş and Gaziantep.

100
Eastern Anatolia
Private Collection, London
1.45 × 2.41 m

There is much discussion and debate on the origin of a certain kilim motif which is visually related to the Ottoman fan-shaped carnation, known from tiles and textiles of the 16th century. However, when viewed in the opposite direction, the same motif looks like a small human figure holding two winged motifs, and is thus more related to the ancient goddess holding two vultures.

In this old kilim, from the Kars region in northeast Anatolia, the debt to Ottoman art is made more obvious by the long tulip-like forms placed inside the petals of the 'carnations'. Nevertheless, the motif has been adapted to the weavers' traditional style, for, while the petals should normally curve inward, here the weaver has added tail-like, outward-curving hooks. This process of assimilation of a court motif to the popular level is further attested by the small triangles and the hooked motifs scattered in the main field, as well as the saw-tooth diamonds in the borders which clearly belong to the traditional repertoire of kilim designs.

I believe that of all the kilims with this design, this piece is the most closely related to the Ottoman carnations. In contrast, there is one kilim in the Fine Arts Museums of San Francisco (C. Cootner, *Anatolian Kilims, the Caroline & H. McCoy Jones Collection*, London 1990, pl. 60) which is more related to the ancient goddess with vultures form.

PUBLISHED:

Y. Petsopoulos, *Kilims*, London 1979, pl. 271.

THE PLATES

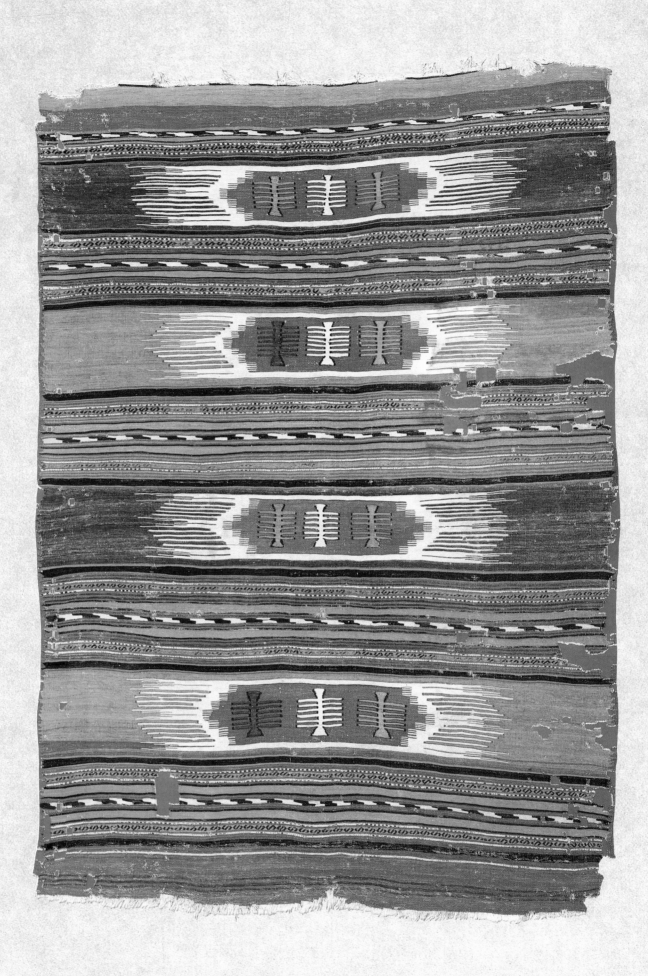

2 $\overline{1.77 \times 2.64 \text{m}}$

1.53 × 2.90m 3

4 $\overline{1.58 \times 2.70\text{m}}$

1.77 × 3.10m **5**

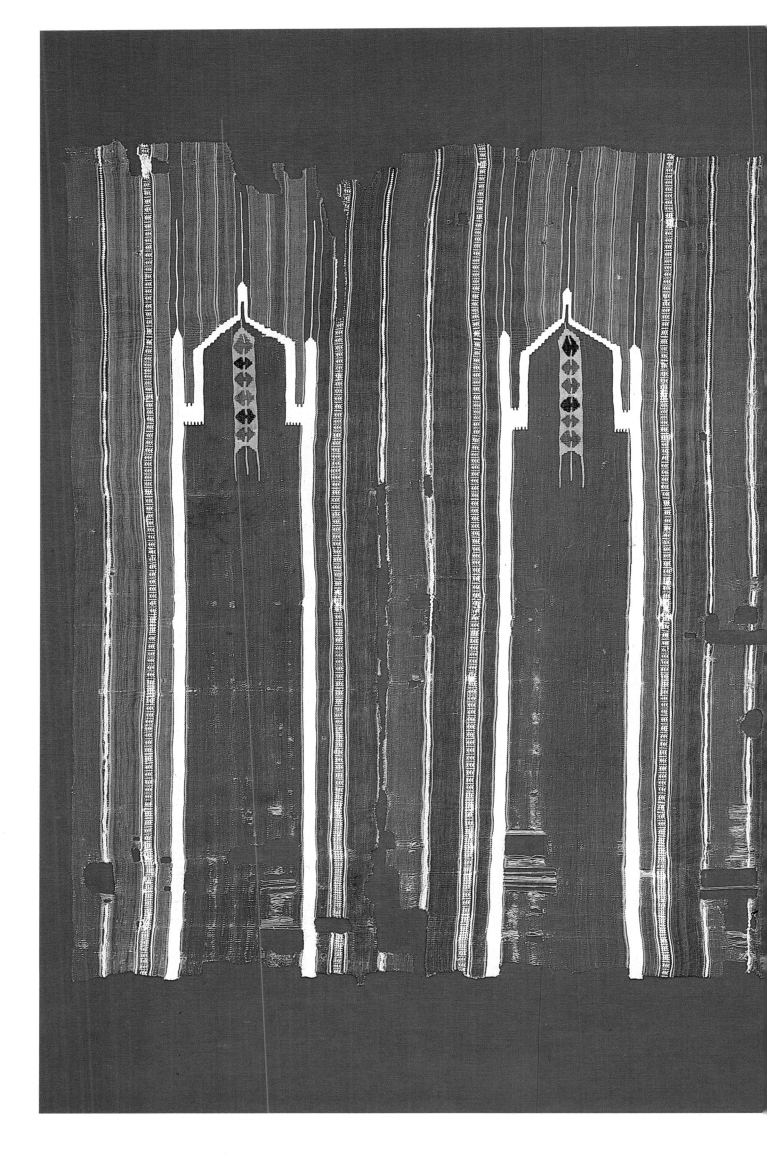

1.27×2.11m

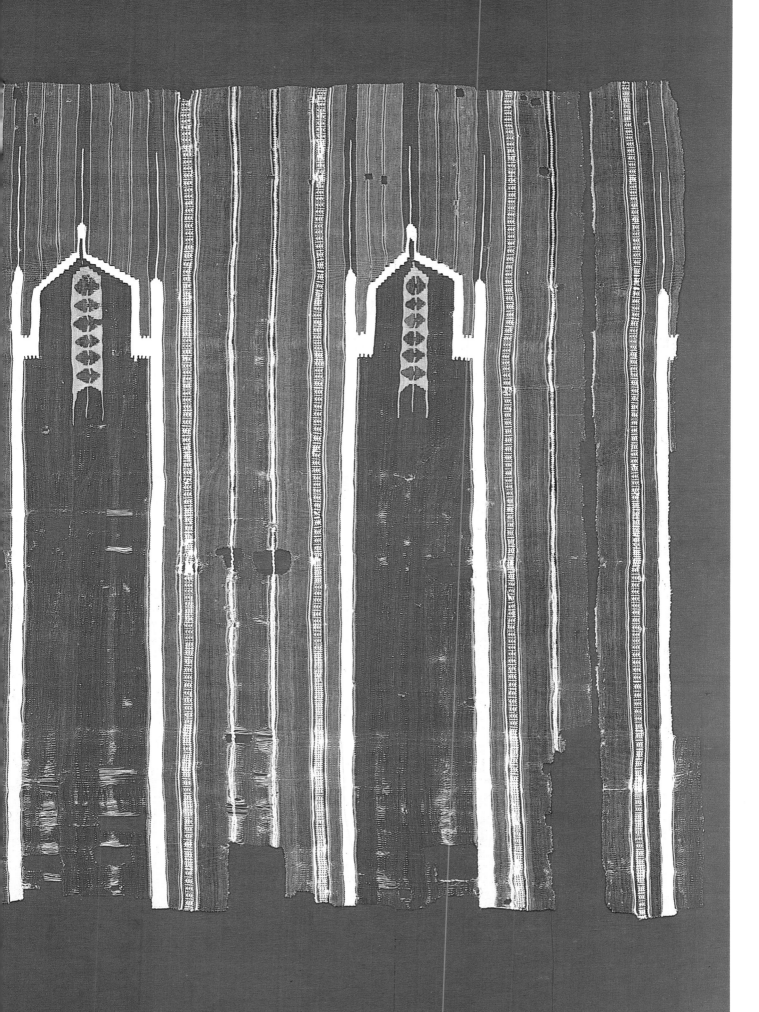

7 1.46 × 3.26m

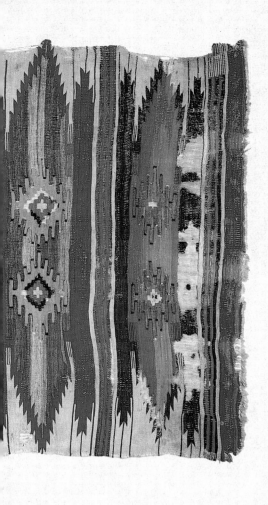

1.682×3.15m **8**

1.36 × 3.25m

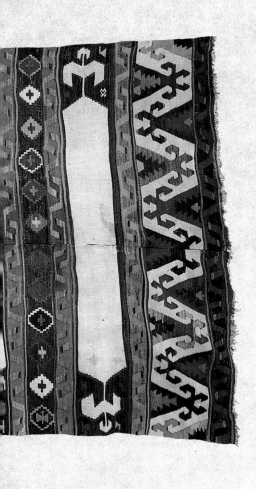

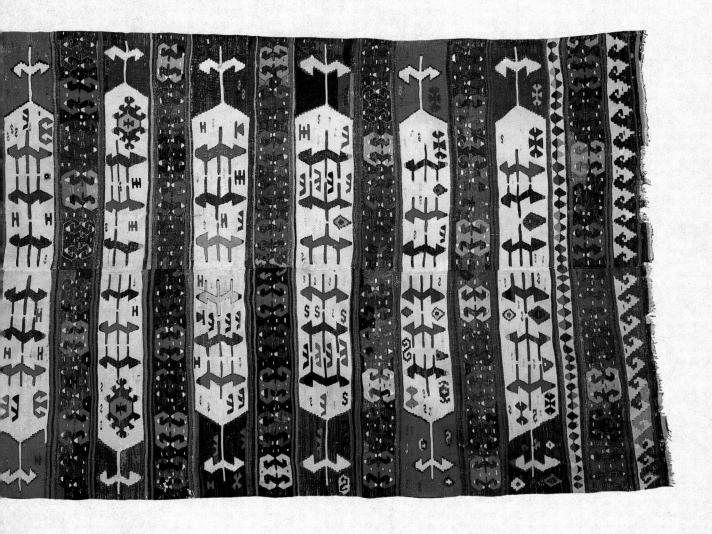

1.65×3.04m 10

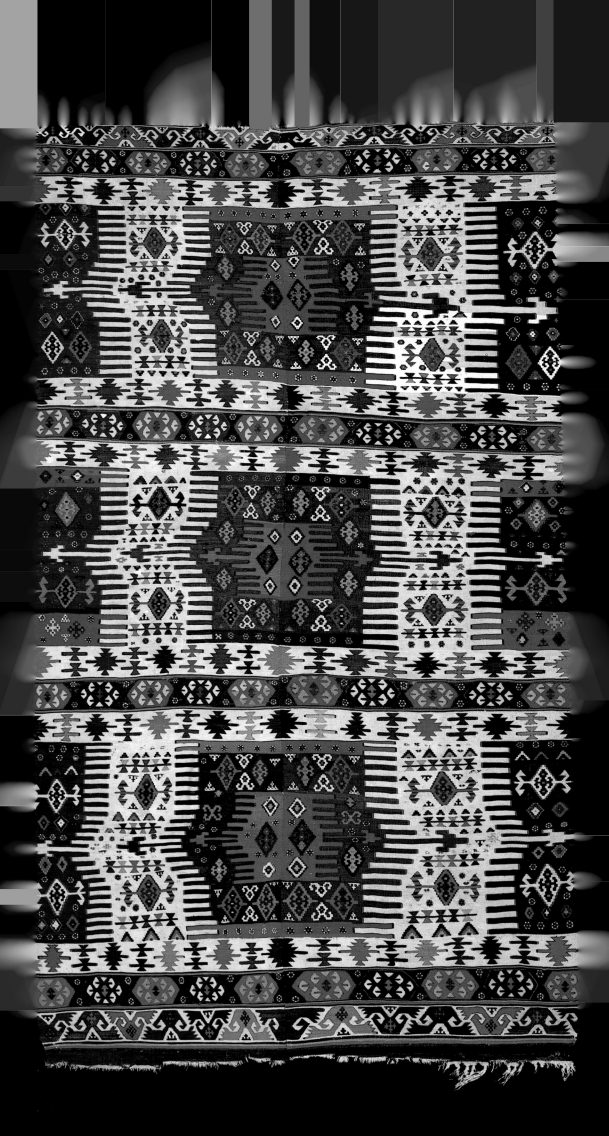

13 <u>1.32 × 2.30m</u>

15 0.87 x 2.22m

17 $\overline{1.58 \times 2.21\text{m}}$

19 $\overline{1.60 \times 2.11m}$

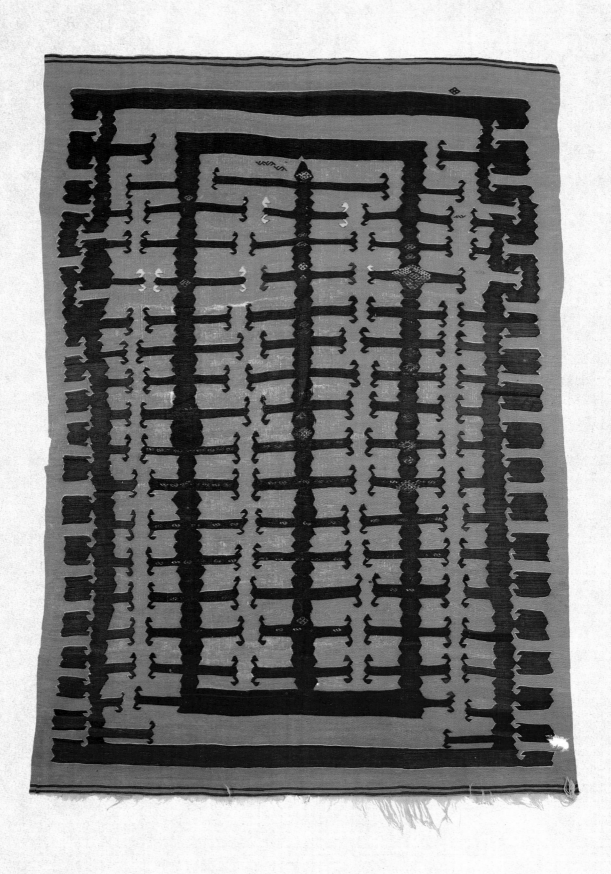

21 $\overline{1.62 \times 2.35m}$

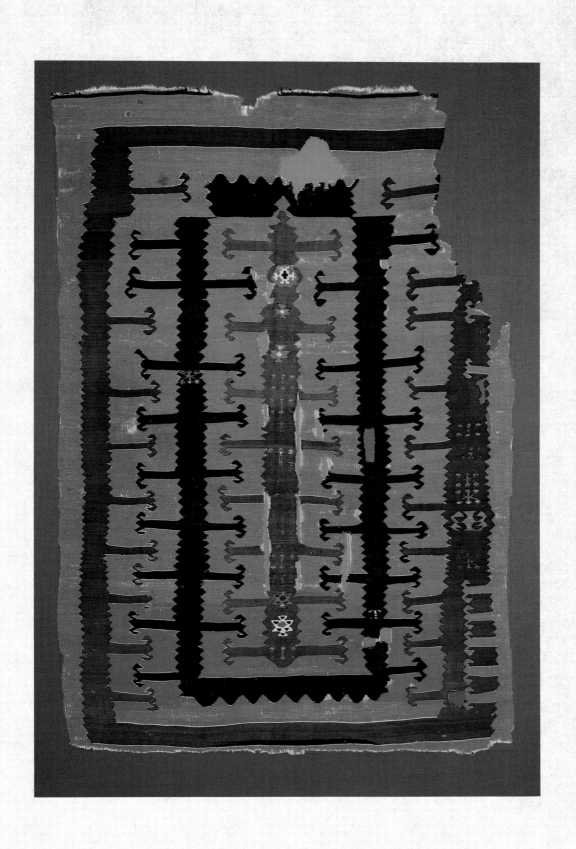

$\overline{1.09 \times 3.55\text{m}}$ **37**

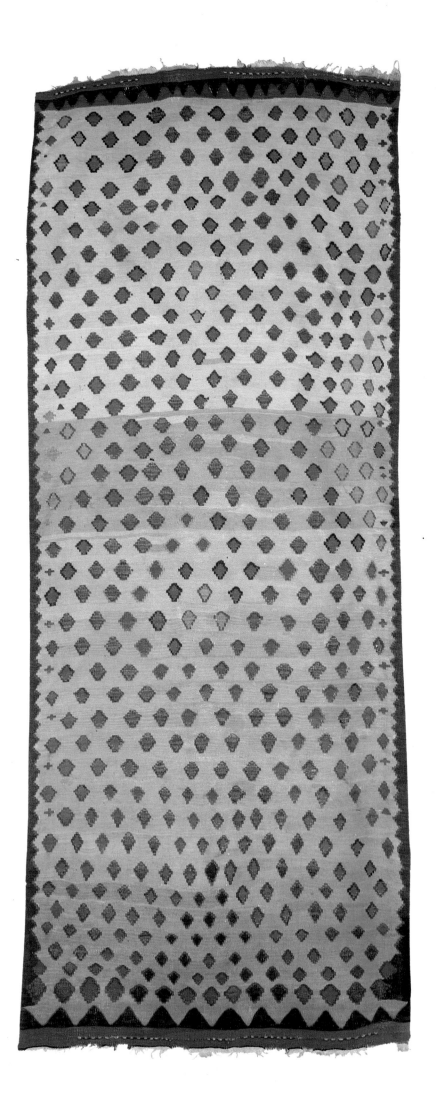

38 1.40 × 3.53m

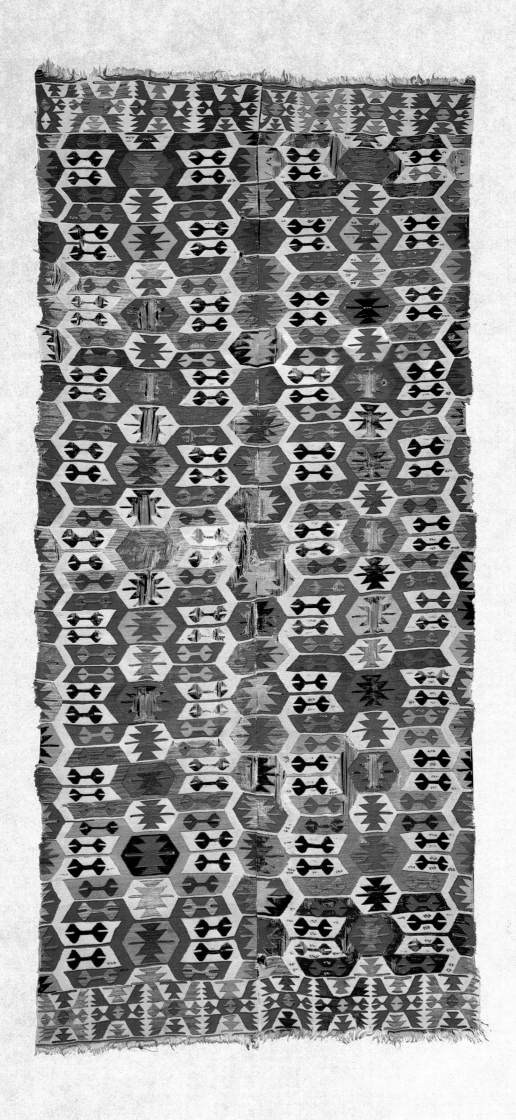

40 1.61×3.66m

1.68×3.71m **43**

44 1.55×3.76m

1.76×2.65m

48 1.47×2.58m

50 <u>1.82 × 3.50m</u>

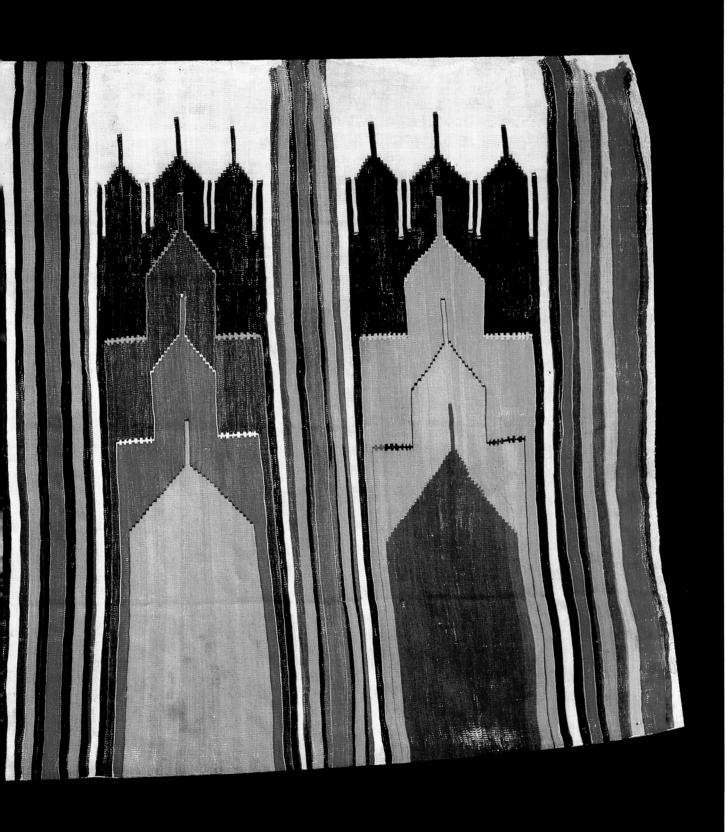

51 $\overline{1.36 \times 3.65m}$

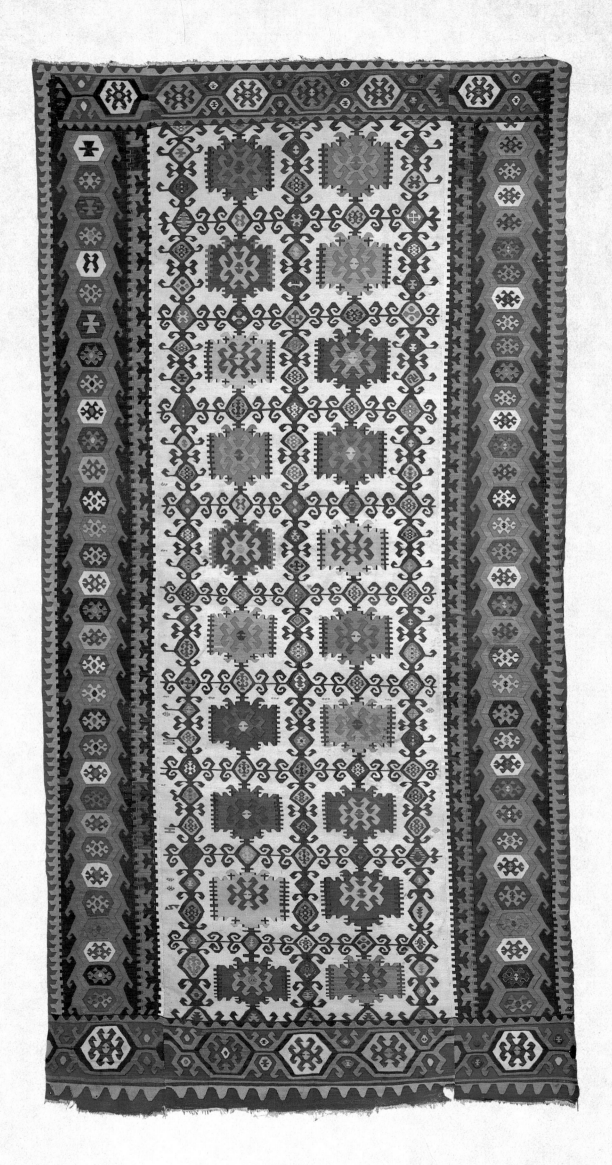

1.88 × 3.98m 52

53 1.50 × 2.40m

1.52 × 3.89m **54**

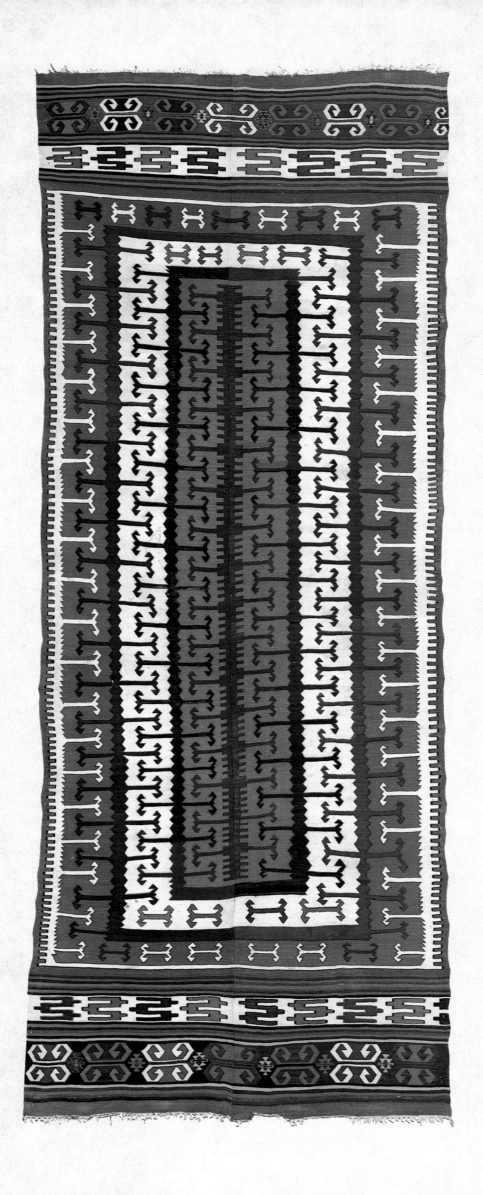

$\overline{1.44 \times 3.76m}$

1.58 × 3.99m 56

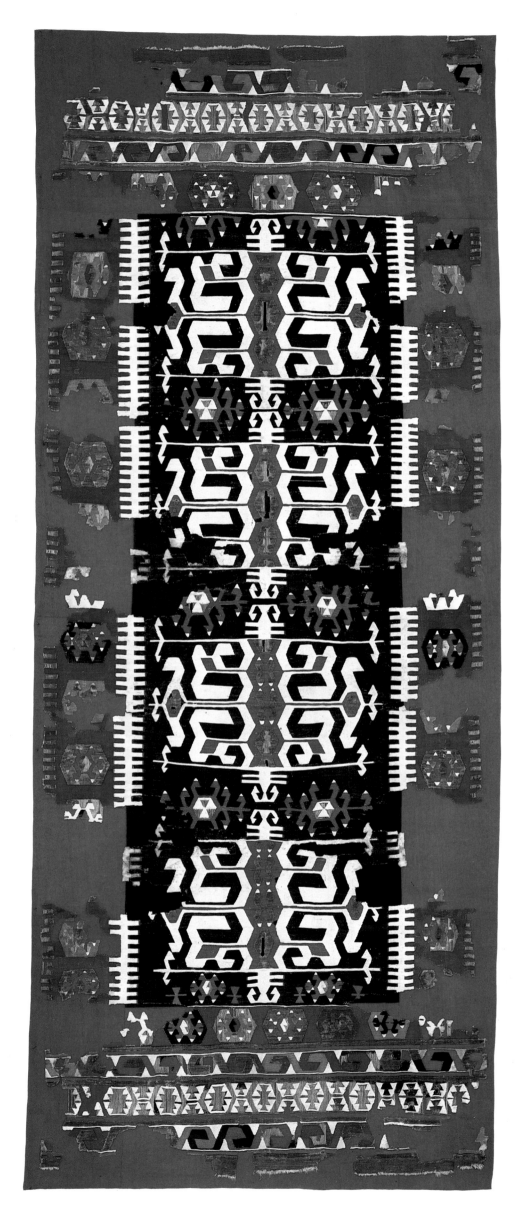

57 1.63 × 4.06m

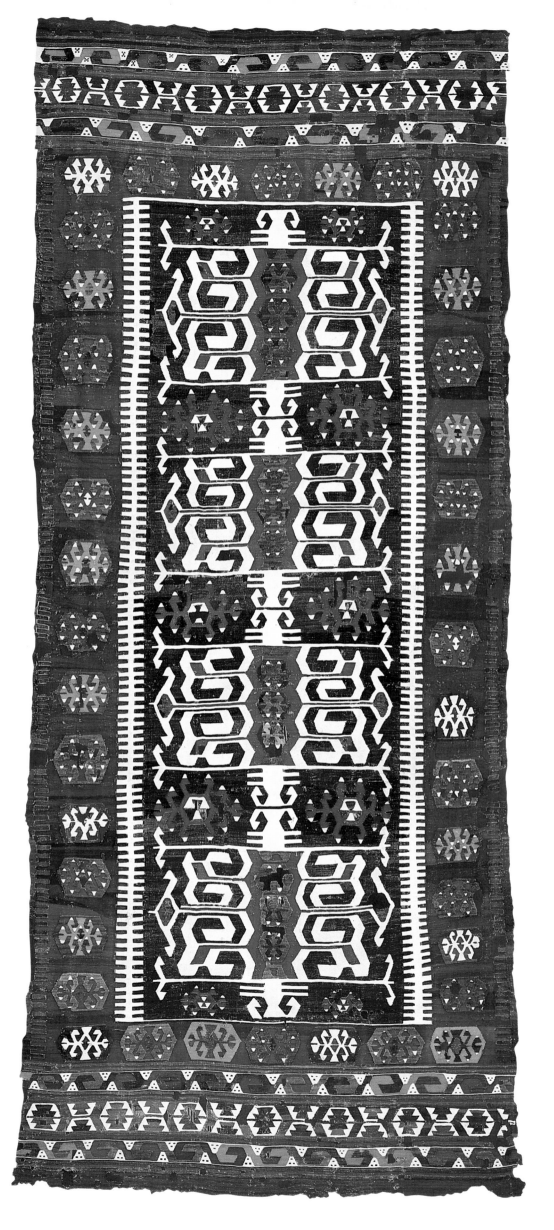

<space start="t="" />1.68 × 4.12m **58**

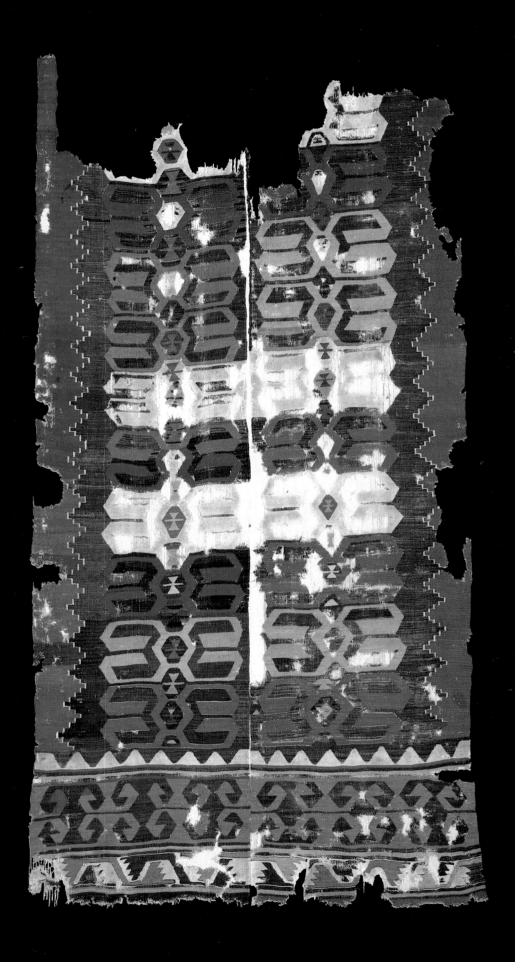

1.58 × 2.95m

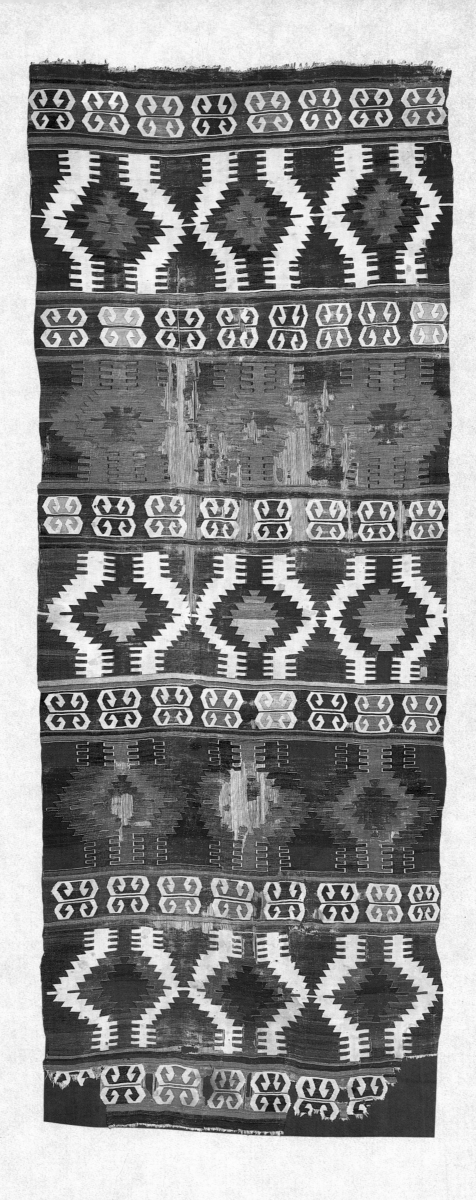

61 1.50 × 4.01 m

63 1.45×3.00m

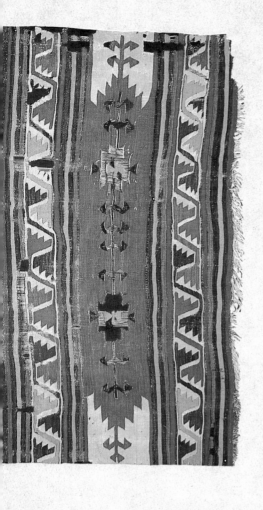

65 1.73 × 4.60m

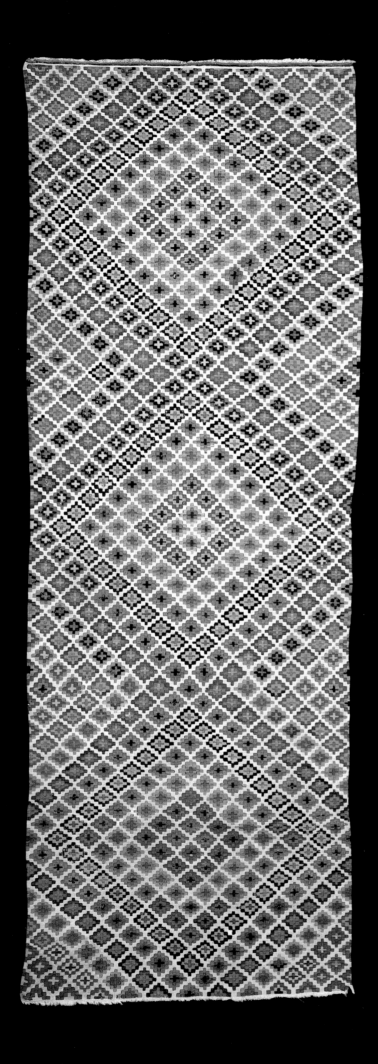

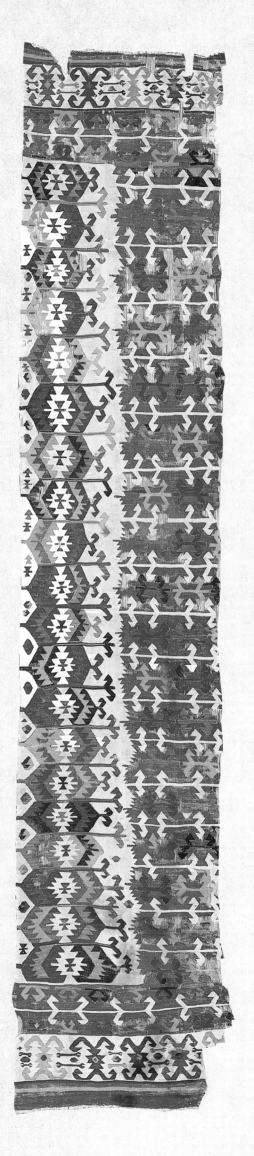

71 1.50×4.15m

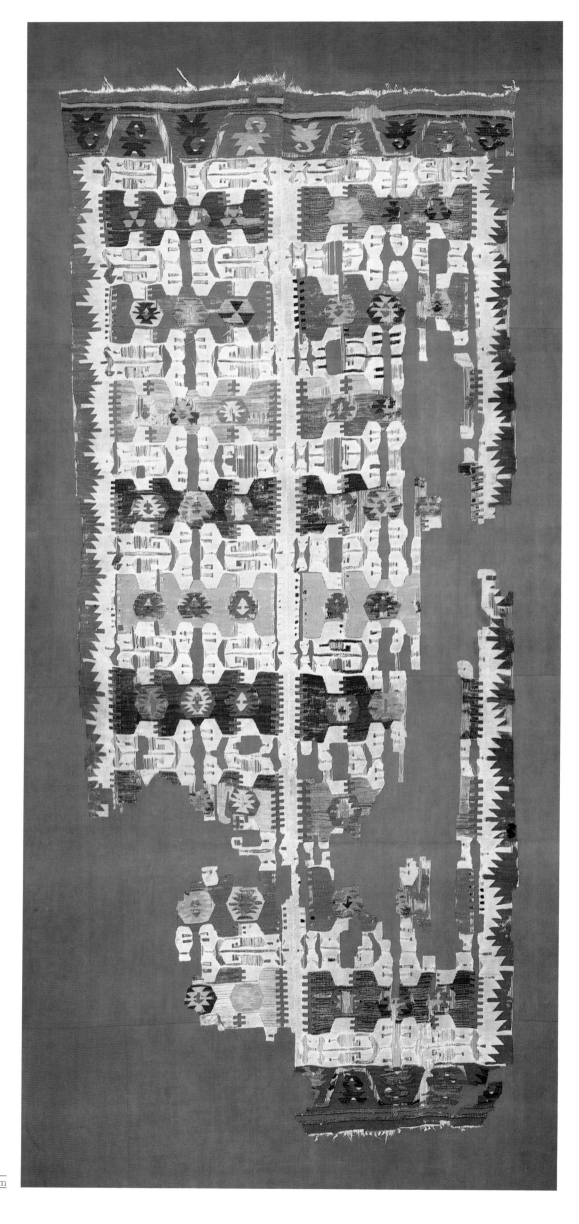

1.88 × 4.24m

77 1.78×3.61m

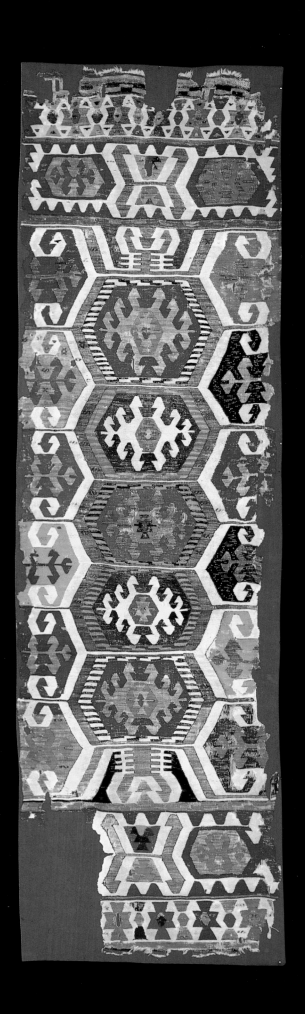

0.90×3.25m **78**

79 1.58 × 3.50m

81 <u>1.55×3.55m</u>

83 <u>1.49×3.73m</u>

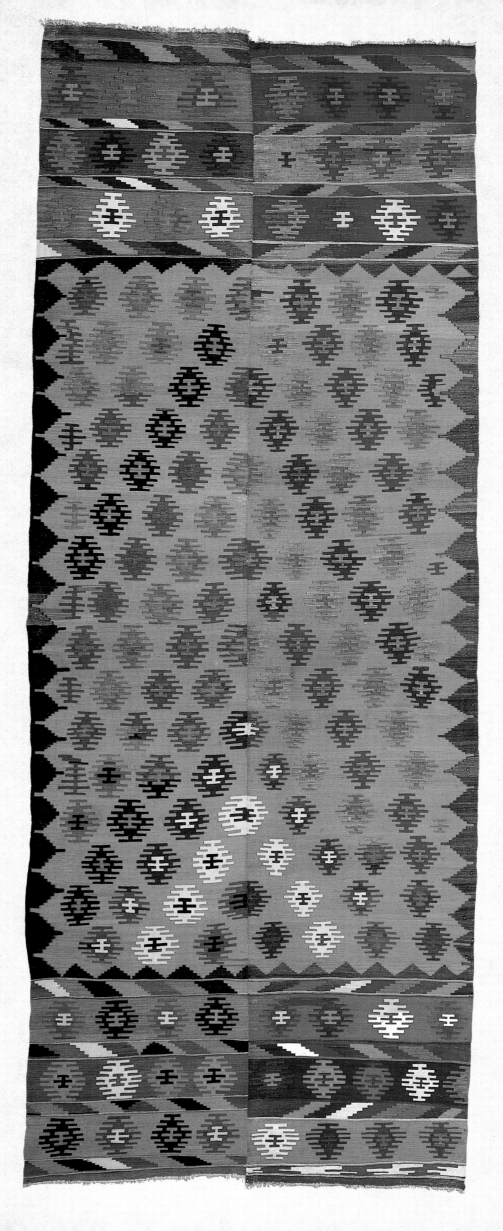

1.60×3.84m

1.42×3.77m

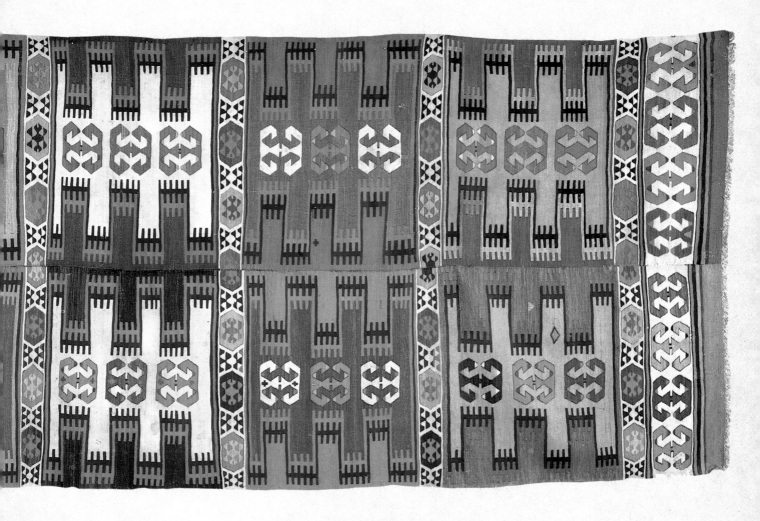

1.57×3.88m

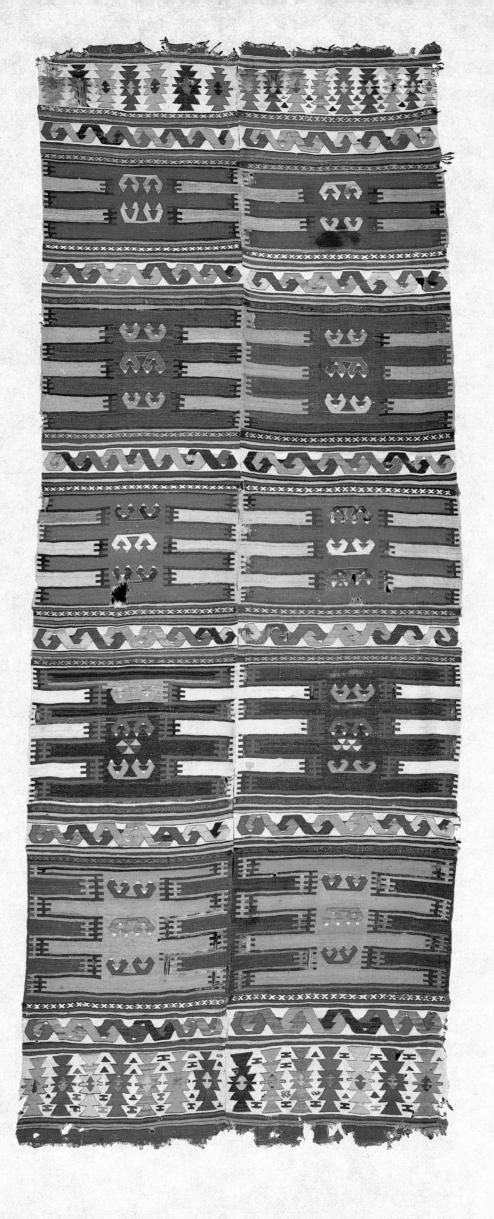

1.57 × 4.07m **89**

1.44 × 1.70m **91**

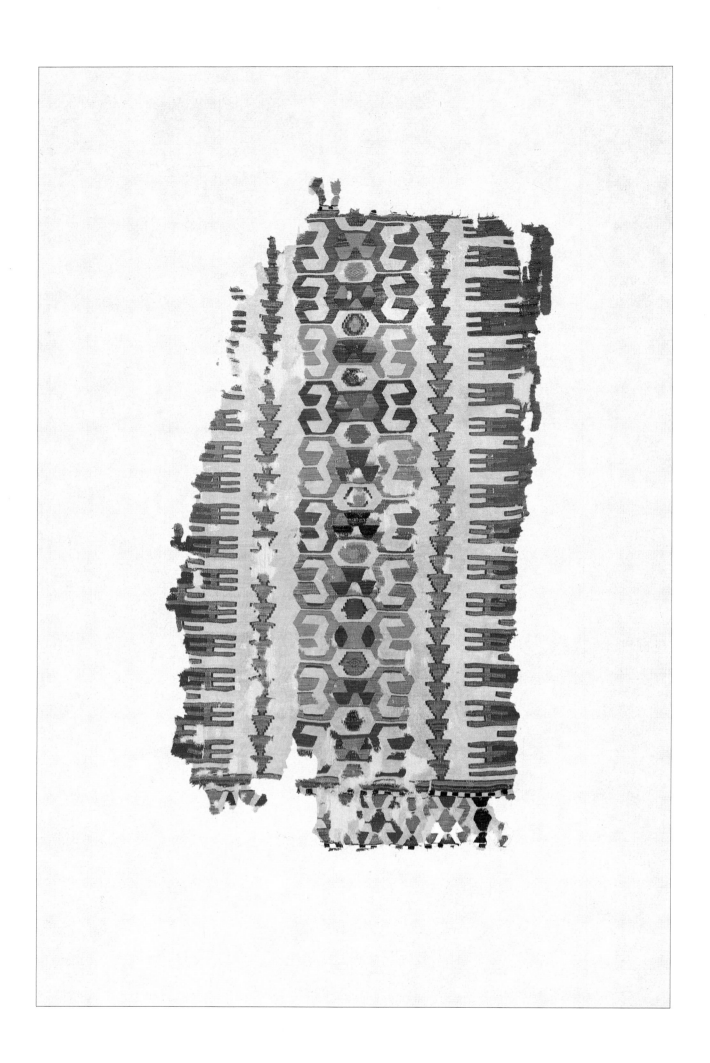

94 $\overline{1.15 \times 2.09\text{m}}$

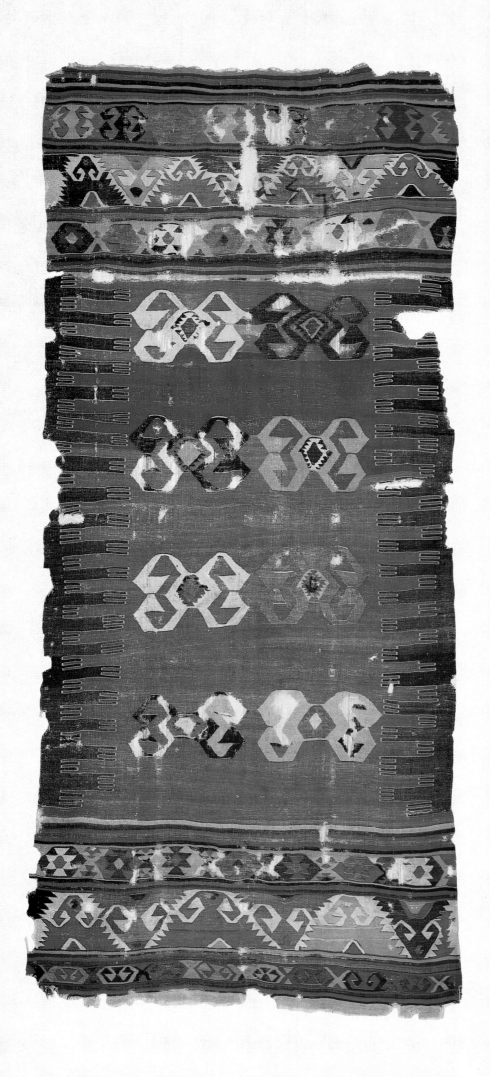

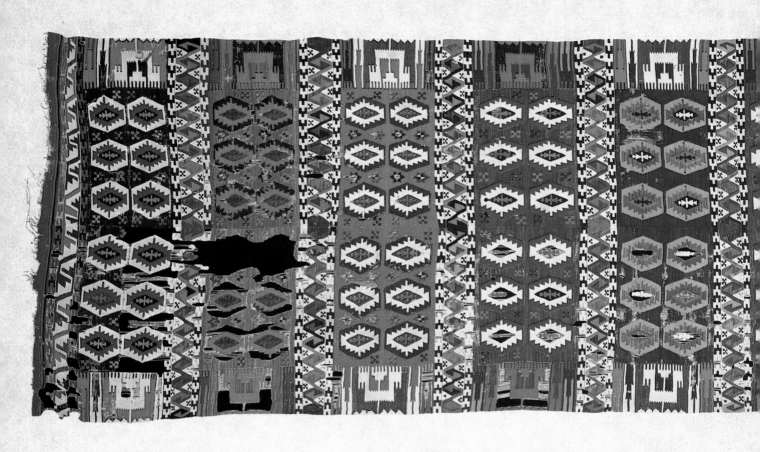

97 1.74 x 4.66m

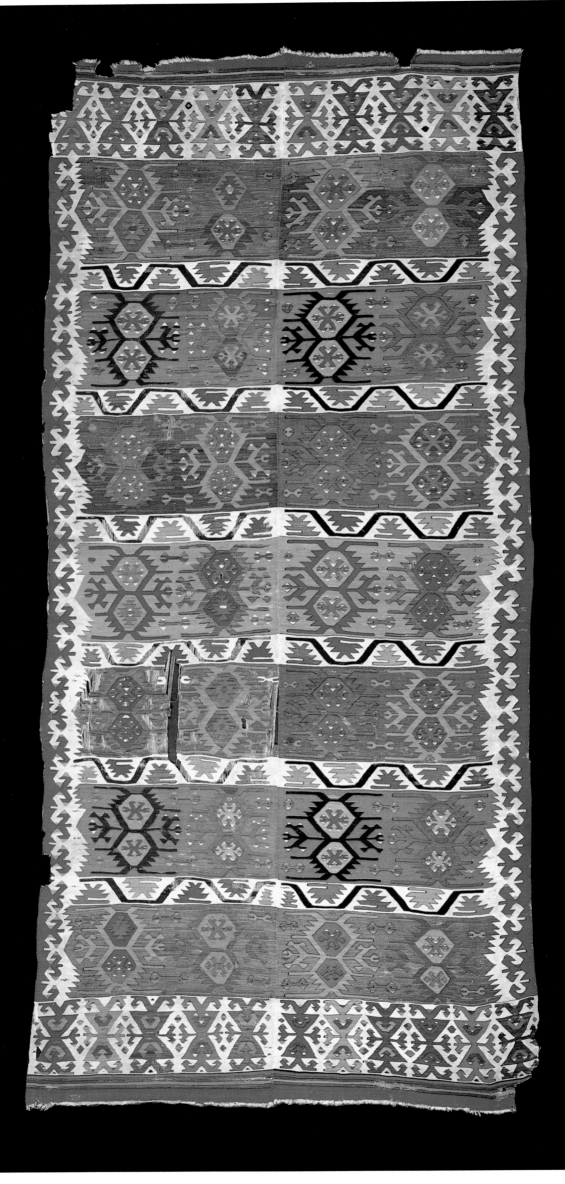

100 $\overline{1.45 \times 2.41\text{m}}$

PHOTOGRAPHIC CREDITS

Selected Bibliography

ACAR (Balpınar), Belkis. 'Yüncü Nomad Weaving in the Balıkesir Region of Western Turkey', in *Yörük, The Nomadic Weaving of the Middle East*, Landreau, Anthony N., ed., Pittsburgh 1978.

ACAR (Balpınar), Belkis. 'The Rugs of the Yüncü Nomads', in *HALI*, vol. 2, no. 2, 1979, pp. 118–120.

ALLEN, Max. *The Birth Symbol in Traditional Women's Art from Eurasia and the Western Pacific*, Toronto Museum of Textiles, 1981.

BALPINAR, Belkis and HIRSCH, Udo. *Flatweaves of the Vakıflar Museum, Istanbul*, Wesel 1982.

BALPINAR, Belkis. 'Some Anatolian Kilims and the Historical Context of their Weavers', in *Anatolian Kilims*, Eskenazi, John, ed., Milan 1984.

BALPINAR, Belkis and HIRSCH, Udo. 'Parmaklı Kilims', in *HALI*, no. 26, 1985, pp. 12–17.

BALPINAR, Belkis. 'A Discussion on Central Asian Türkmen Influence on Anatolian Kilims', in *Oriental Carpet and Textile Studies*, vol. 3, no. 2, 1989, pp. 7–17.

BALPINAR, Belkis. 'Anatolian Kilims, Past and Present', in Mellaart, James; Hirsch, Udo and Balpınar, Belkis. *The Goddess from Anatolia*, Milan 1989, vol. IV.

BALPINAR, Belkis. 'Multiple-niche Kilims within their Historical Context', in Rageth, Jürg, ed., *Anatolische Kelims, Symposium Basel, Die Vorträge*, Basel 1990, pp. 83–93.

BARTELS, Herwig. 'Anatolische Flachgewebe', in *Kunst & Antiquitäten*, vol. 1, 1985.

BARTELS, Herwig. 'On the Origins of Anatolian Kilim Designs', in *Oriental Carpet and Textile Studies*, vol. I, 1985, pp. 202–210.

BARTELS, Herwig. 'Y.P. 153: a Central Anatolian Kilim', in Connoisseur's Choice, *HALI*, no. 36, 1987.

BAUSBACK, Peter. *Alte Orientalische Flachgewebe*, Mannheim 1977.

BAUSBACK, Peter. *Alte und Antike Orientalische Flachgewebe*, Mannheim 1982.

BAUSBACK, Peter. *Kelim, Antike Orientalische Flachgewebe*, Munich 1983.

BELLINGER, Louisa. 'Textiles from Gordion', in *The Bulletin of the Needle and Bobbin Club*, 46, 1962, pp. 4–33.

BLACK, David & LOVELESS, Clive, eds. *The Undiscovered Kilim*, London 1977.

BODE, Wilhelm von and KÜHNEL, Ernst. *Antique Rugs from the Near East*, London 1970.

BRÜGGEMANN, Werner. 'Carpets and Kilims – a Contribution to the Problem of the Origin of Designs in Kilims', in *Oriental Carpet and Textile Studies*, vol. 3, no. 2, 1989.

BURCKHARDT, Titus. *Alchemy*, London 1967.

BURCKHARDT, Titus. *Sacred Art in East and West*, London 1967.

CASSIN, Jack. *Image, Idol, Symbol, Ancient Anatolian Kelims*, New York 1989.

COOTNER, Cathryn M. *Anatolian Kilims, The Caroline & H. McCoy Jones Collection*, London 1990.

CRITCHLOW, Keith. *Order in Space*, London 1969.

CRITCHLOW, Keith. *Islamic Pattern*, London 1976.

DENNY, Walter B. 'Links between Anatolian Kilim Designs and Older Traditions', in *HALI*, vol. 2, no. 2, 1979, pp. 105–109.

DENNY, Walter B. 'Saff and Sejjadeh, Origins and Meaning of the Prayer Rug', in *Oriental Carpet Studies*, vol. 3, no. 2, 1989, pp. 93–104.

DODDS, Dennis. 'Anatolian Kilims from the Sivas Region', in *HALI*, vol. 1, no. 4, 1978, pp. 319–324.

ELIADE, Mircea. *Myth and Reality*, New York 1963.

ELLIS, Charles Grant. 'The Rugs of the Great Mosque Divrik', in *HALI*, vol. 1, no. 3, 1978, pp. 269–279.

EMERY, Irene. *The Primary Structures of Fabrics*, Washington, D.C. 1966.

ENDERLEIN, Volkmar. *Orientalische Kelims: Flachgewebe aus Anatolien, den Kaukasus und dem Iran*, Wesel 1986.

ERBEK, Güran. *Kilim Catalogue No. 1*, Ankara 1988.

ESKENAZI, John. *Kilim*, Milan 1980.

ESKENAZI, John, ed. *Kilim anatolici; Anatolian kilims*, Milan 1984.

ESKENAZI, John & VALCARENGHI, Dario, eds. *Kilim Anatolici*, Milan 1985.

FRANSES, Michael and MARCUSON, Alan. *Kilims, the Traditional Tapestries of Turkey*, Dublin 1979.

FRAUENKNECHT, Bertram. *Anatolische Kelims; Anatolian Kilims*, Nürnberg 1982.

FRAUENKNECHT, Bertram. *Frühe Türkische Tapisserien; Early Turkish Tapestries*, Nürnberg 1984.

GÖNÜL, Macide. 'Türk Halı ve Kilimlerinin Teknik Hususiyetleri', in *Türk Etnoğrafya Dergisi*, no. 2, Ankara 1957.

GÖNÜL, Macide. 'Türk Halı ve Kilimlerinde Sembolik Kuş Şekilleri', in *Dil ve Tarih Coğrafya Fakültesi Antropoloji Dergisi*, Ankara 1965.

GUENON, René. *Symboles Fondamentaux de la Science Sacrée*, Paris 1962.

GUENON, René. 'Initiation and the Crafts', in *Journal of the Indian Society of Oriental Art*, vol. VI, 1938.

HIRSCH, Udo. 'Environment, Economy, Cult and Culture', in Mellaart, James; Hirsch, Udo and Balpınar, Belkis. *The Goddess from Anatolia*, Milan 1989, vol. III.

KOLLER, Galerie. Auction 19, Zürich, March 1988.

LINGS, Martin. *Ancient Beliefs and Modern Superstitions*, London 1965.

MELLAART, James. *The Neolithic of the Near East*, London 1975.

MELLAART, James. 'Çatal Hüyük and Anatolian Kilims', in Mellaart, James; Hirsch, Udo and Balpınar, Belkis. *The Goddess from Anatolia*, Milan 1989, vol. II.

MELLAART, James; HIRSCH, Udo and BALPINAR, Belkis. *The Goddess from Anatolia*, Milan 1989.

ÖLÇER, Nazan. *Kilims*, Turkish and Islamic Art Museum, Istanbul 1988.

PETSOPOULOS, Yanni. *In Praise of Allah,*

Prayer Kilims from the Near East, London 1975.

PETSOPOULOS, Yanni. Catalogue section in Black, David and Loveless, Clive, eds., *The Undiscovered Kilim*, London 1977.

PETSOPOULOS, Yanni. *Kilims*, London 1979.

PETSOPOULOS, Yanni. 'Kilims, a 10th Anniversary Reappraisal', in Rageth, Jürg, ed., *Anatolische Kelims, Symposium Basel, Die Vorträge*, Basel 1990, pp. 49–54.

PETSOPOULOS, Yanni. *From the Danube to the Euphrates, Kilims of the 18th and 19th Centuries*, Athens 1990.

PLOIER, Helmut. *Gewebte Poesie, Sammlung Konzett*, Graz 1991.

POWELL, Josephine. 'An Argument for the Origins of Anatolian Kilim Designs', in *Oriental Carpet and Textile Studies*, vol. 3, no. 2, 1989.

RAGETH, Jürgen. *Kilim, Simboli Primitivi della Mitologia; Kilim, Primitive Symbols of Mythology*, Rome 1986.

RAGETH, Jürg, ed. *Anatolische Kelims, Symposium Basel, die Vorträge*, Basel 1990.

RUMI. *Mathnawi*, London 1925–1940.

SAILER, Galerie. *Aus der Welt des Kelim; The World of the Kilim*, Vienna 1984.

VOLKMANN, Martin, ed. *Alte Orientteppiche; Old Eastern Carpets, Masterpieces in German Private Collections*, Munich 1985.

WATERHOUSE, Davina. 'Orphans of the Art World', in *HALI*, vol. 7, no. 2, 1985.

YETKIN, Şerare. 'Divriği Ulu Cami'inde Bulunan Osmanlı Saray Sanatı Üslübundaki Kilimler', in *Belleten*, vol. XLII, no. 165, 1978.

ZIEMBA, William; AKATAY, Abdulkadir and SCHWARTZ, Sandra. *Turkish Flatweaves*, London 1979.

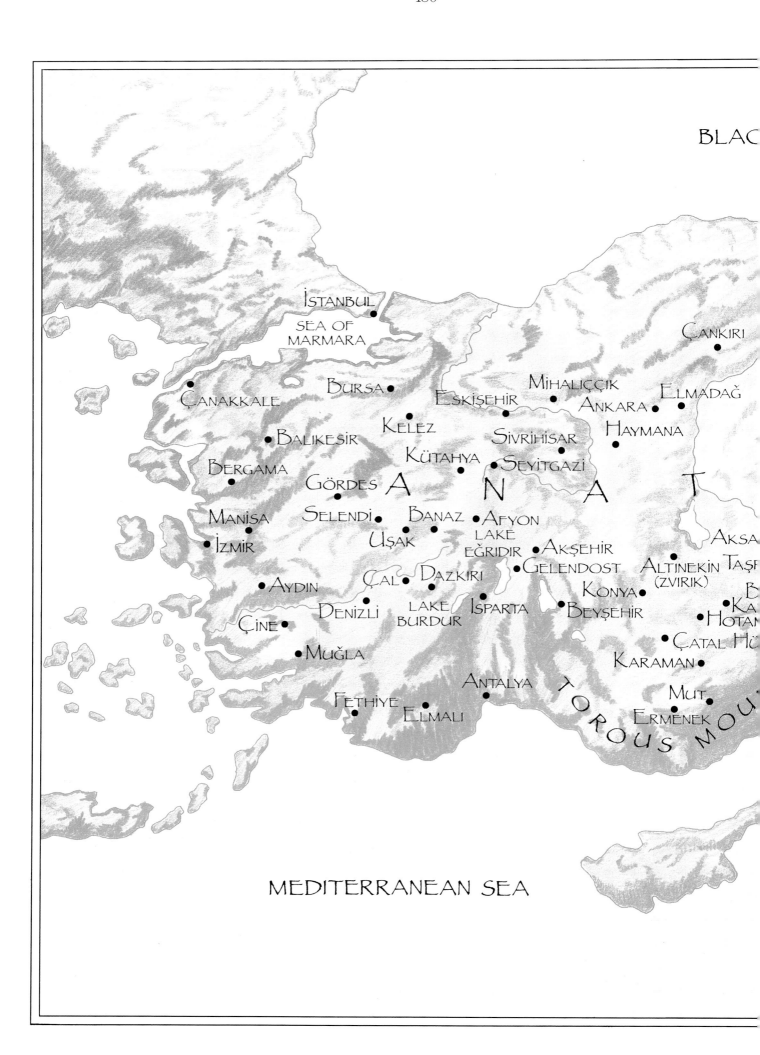

BLAC

İSTANBUL

SEA OF
MARMARA

ÇANKIRI

ÇANAKKALE

BURSA

ESKİŞEHİR

MİHALIÇÇIK

ANKARA

ELMADAĞ

KELEZ

SİVRİHİSAR

HAYMANA

BALIKESİR

KÜTAHYA

SEYİTGAZİ

BERGAMA

GÖRDES

A

N

A

T

MANİSA

SELENDİ

BANAZ

AFYON

İZMİR

UŞAK

LAKE
EĞRİDİR

AKSA

AKŞEHİR

ALTINEKİN TAŞ
(ZVIRIK)

AYDIN

ÇAL

DAZKIRI

GELENDOST

KONYA

B
KA

DENİZLİ

LAKE
BURDUR

ISPARTA

BEYŞEHİR

HOTAM

ÇİNE

ÇATAL Hü

MUĞLA

KARAMAN

ANTALYA

TOROUS MOU

MUT

FETHİYE

ELMALI

ERMENEK

MEDITERRANEAN SEA

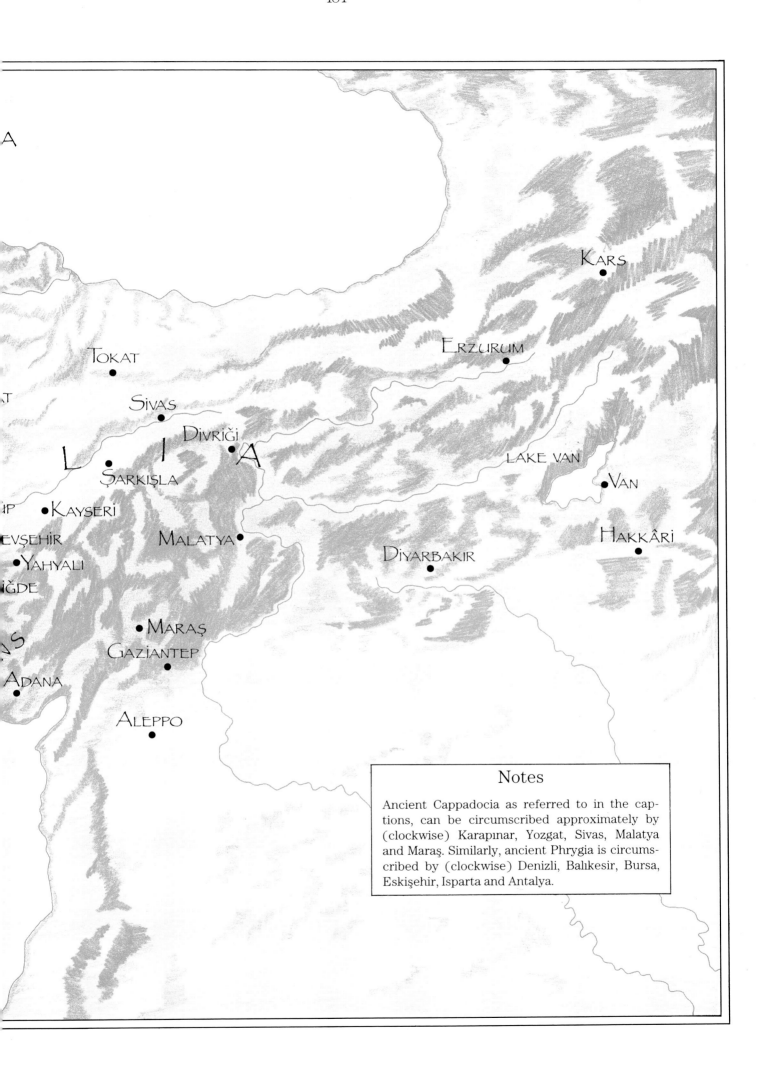

Notes

Ancient Cappadocia as referred to in the captions, can be circumscribed approximately by (clockwise) Karapınar, Yozgat, Sivas, Malatya and Maraş. Similarly, ancient Phrygia is circumscribed by (clockwise) Denizli, Balıkesir, Bursa, Eskişehir, Isparta and Antalya.

Index

Numbers in italics indicate the captions. All other numbers refer to the pages.